# US ARMY FIELD MANUAL 5-20

# CAMOUFLAGE, CONCEALMENT, & DECOYS

# NOVEMBER, 2010

**Battles & Book Reviews Publishing**

All content in this work except the Editor's Note and clearly marked text box
inclusions are public domain

ISBN: 1543182372
ISBN-13: 978-1543182378

Army Tactics, Techniques, and Procedures

No. 3-34.39/Marine Corps Reference Publication 3-17.6A

Headquarters

Department of the Army

Washington, DC, 26 November 2010

Camouflage, Concealment, and Decoys

# TABLE OF CONTENTS

# EDITOR'S NOTE

This volume contains the November 2010 version of US Army **Field Manual 5-20 Camouflage, Concealment, & Decoys.**

Unlike many of the older manuals this manual is not chock full of illustrations and instructions on how to build and/or camouflage military positions. This is a much more cerebral and informative book that spends a lot of effort explaining the theory of camouflage on the modern battlefield and discussing methods to defeat it. This is important information in an era when infrared, satellite, and thermal optics and sensors can be bought on the civilian market. In the modern era it is not enough to just throw some dirt and realistic looking vegetation over a position or structure in order to stay hidden, you have to account for electromagnetic and other emissions that are invisible to the naked eye but stand out like a beacon to modern sensors. During my military career I was continually amazed at the resolution and detection abilities of the equipment we used. Even the slightest light is visible at great distances with even 1st Generation light enhancers, you can see the cherry from a cigarette at a couple of kilometers with such equipment and the newer generation image intensifiers are even better than the stuff I first used 25+ years ago. An appreciation for the sophistication of modern sensors is just one of the takeaways from this manual.

I have modified this copy somewhat by simplifying the table of contents. As with all the other US Army manuals I am making available as hardcopies I have also renumbered the pages to be consecutive throughout the book instead of the weird chapter numbering system the military uses and that I always hated. Instead of going through the manual and cherry picking and publishing only the info that I thought would be useful I have left the manual complete so that you, the individual, can be the judge of what information is useful to you and what is not.

I have attempted to fix all page references to reflect the new numbering but it is entirely possible that I have missed one or more. My goal in compiling these was to make them available at an affordable price using modern Print-On-Demand (POD) technology. I hope these manuals are instructive.

If you discover any typos or incorrect references please send an email to info@military-history.us with the mistake and which page it is on so I can fix it in subsequent releases.

# PREFACE

This Army Tactics, Techniques, and Procedures (ATTP) is intended to help company-level leaders understand the principles and techniques of camouflage, concealment, and decoys (CCD). To remain viable, all units must apply CCD to personnel and equipment. Ignoring a threat's ability to detect friendly operations on the battlefield is shortsighted and dangerous. Friendly units enhance their survivability capabilities if they are well versed in CCD principles and techniques.

CCD is equal in importance to marksmanship, maneuver, and mission. It is an integral part of a soldier's duty. CCD encompasses individual and unit efforts such as movement, light, and noise discipline; letter control; dispersal; and deception operations. Each soldier's actions must contribute to the unit's overall CCD posture to maximize effectiveness.

Increased survivability is the goal of a CCD plan. A unit commander must encourage each soldier to think of survivability and CCD as synonymous terms. Training soldiers to recognize this correlation instills a greater appreciation of CCD values.

A metric conversion chart is provided in Appendix A.

This publication applies to the Active Army, Army National Guard (ARNG)/Army National Guard of the United States (ARNGUS), and the United States Army Reserve (USAR) unless otherwise stated.

The proponent of this publication is United States Army Training and Doctrine Command (TRADOC). Send comments and recommendations of Department of the Army (DA) Form 2028 (Recommended Changes to Publications and Blank Forms) directly to Commandant, United States Army Engineer School (USAES), ATTN: ATSE-DOT-DD, Fort Leonard Wood, Missouri 65473-6650.

This publication implements Standardization Agreement (STANAG) 2931, Orders for the Camouflage of the Red Cross and Red Crescent on Land in Tactical Operations.

Unless otherwise stated, masculine nouns and pronouns do not refer exclusively to men.

# CHAPTER 1 – BASICS

CCD is the use of materials and techniques to hide, blend, disguise, decoy, or disrupt the appearance of military targets and/or their backgrounds. CCD helps prevent an enemy from detecting or identifying friendly troops, equipment, activities, or installations. Properly designed CCD techniques take advantage of the immediate environment and natural and artificial materials. One of the imperatives of current military doctrine is to conserve friendly strength for decisive action. Such conservation is aided through sound operations security (OPSEC) and protection from attack. Protection includes all actions that make soldiers, equipment, and units difficult to locate.

## Doctrinal Considerations

1-1. CCD degrades the effectiveness of enemy reconnaissance, surveillance, and target-acquisition (RSTA) capabilities. Skilled observers and sophisticated sensors can be defeated by obscuring telltale signs (signatures) of units on the battlefield. Preventing detection impairs enemy efforts to assess friendly operational patterns, functions, and capabilities.

1-2. CCD enhances friendly survivability by reducing an enemy's ability to detect, identify, and engage friendly elements. Survivability encompasses all actions taken to conserve personnel, facilities, and supplies from the effects of enemy weapons and actions. Survivability techniques include using physical measures such as fighting and protective positions; nuclear, biological, chemical (NBC) equipment; and armor. These actions include interrelated tactical countermeasures such as dispersion, movement techniques, OPSEC, communications security (COMSEC), CCD, and smoke operations (a form of CCD). Improved survivability from CCD is not restricted to combat operations. Benefits are also derived by denying an enemy the collection of information about friendly forces during peacetime.

1-3. Deception helps mask the real intent of primary combat operations and aids in achieving surprise. Deception countermeasures can delay effective enemy reaction by disguising information about friendly intentions, capabilities, objectives, and locations of vulnerable units and facilities. Conversely, intentionally poor CCD can project misleading information about friendly operations. Successful tactical deception depends on stringent OPSEC.

1-4. Smoke and obscurants are effective CCD tools and greatly enhance the effectiveness of other traditionally passive CCD techniques. Smoke and obscurants can change battlefield dynamics by blocking or degrading the spectral bands used by an enemy's target-acquisition and weapons systems. More recently developed obscurants are now able to degrade nonvisual detection systems such as thermal infrared (IR) imaging systems, selected radar systems, and laser systems.

# Responsibilities

1-5. Each soldier is responsible for camouflaging and concealing himself and his equipment. Practicing good CCD techniques lessens a soldier's probability of becoming a target. Additionally, a thorough knowledge of CCD and its guiding principles allows a soldier to easily recognize CCD as employed by an enemy.

1-6. A commander is responsible for CCD of his unit, and noncommissioned officers (NCOs) supervise well-disciplined soldiers in executing CCD. They use established standing operating procedures (SOPs) and battle drills to guide their efforts. CCD is a combat multiplier that should be exploited to the fullest extent.

1-7. An engineer is a battlefield expert on CCD. He integrates CCD into higher unit operations and advises commanders on all aspects of CCD employment as it relates to a unit's current mission.

# Priorities

1-8. Every soldier and military unit has an inherent mission of self-protection, and they should use all CCD means available. However, CCD countermeasures have become more complicated due to advancing technology. Commanders must recognize that advanced technologies have -

- Enhanced the performance of enemy recon and surveillance equipment.
- Increased an enemy's ability to use electromagnetic (EM) signature analysis for detecting friendly units.
- Reduced the time available to apply CCD because units must perform nearly all aspects of battlefield operations at an increased speed.

1-9. When time, camouflage materials, or other resources are insufficient to provide adequate support to units, commanders must prioritize CCD operations. Considerations for establishing these priorities involve analyzing the mission, enemy, terrain, weather, troops, time available, and civilian considerations (METT-TC). The following sets forth a METT-TC methodology to help determine CCD priorities:

- **Mission.** The mission is always the first and most important consideration. CCD efforts must enhance the mission but not be so elaborate that they hinder a unit's ability to accomplish the mission.
- **Enemy.** An enemy's RSTA capabilities often influence the camouflage materials and CCD techniques needed to support a

unit's mission. Before beginning a mission, conduct an intelligence analysis to identify the enemy's RSTA capabilities.

- **Terrain and weather**. The battlefield terrain generally dictates what CCD techniques and materials are necessary. Different terrain types or background environments (urban, mountain, forest, plains, desert, arctic) require specific CCD techniques. (See chapter 7 for more information.)
- **Troops**. Friendly troops must be well trained in CCD techniques that apply to their mission, unit, and equipment. A change in the environment or the mission often requires additional training on effective techniques. Leaders must also consider the alertness of troops. Careless CCD efforts are ineffective and may disclose a unit's location, degrade its survivability, and hamper its mission accomplishment. Intelligence analysis should address the relative detectability of friendly equipment and the target signatures that unit elements normally project.
- **Time**. Time is often a critical consideration. Elaborate CCD may not be practical in all tactical situations. The type and amount of CCD needed are impacted by the time a unit occupies a given area, the time available to employ CCD countermeasures, and the time necessary to remove and reemploy camouflage during unit relocation. Units should continue to improve and perfect CCD measures as time allows.
- **Civilian considerations**. From conflict to war and from tactical to strategic, civilians in the area of operation (AO) may be active or passive collectors of information. Commanders and their staffs should manage this collection capability to benefit the command and the mission.

# Training

1-10. CCD training must be included in every field exercise. Soldiers must be aware that an enemy can detect, identify, and acquire targets by using resources outside the visual portion of the EM spectrum.

### Individual

1-11. Each member of the unit must acquire and maintain critical CCD skills. These include the ability to analyze and use terrain effectively; to select an individual site properly; and to hide, blend, disguise, disrupt, and decoy key signatures using natural and artificial materials.

*CAUTION: Ensure that local environmental considerations are addressed before cutting live vegetation or foliage in training areas.*

1-12. Unit CCD training refines individual and leader skills, introduces the element of team coordination, and contributes to tactical realism. If CCD is to conserve friendly strength, it must be practiced with the highest degree of discipline. The deployment and teardown of camouflage; light, noise, and communications discipline; and signal security must be practiced and evaluated in an integrated mission-training environment. CCD proficiency is developed through practicing and incorporating lessons learned from exercises and operations. A unit must incorporate CCD (who, what, where, when, and how) into its tactical standing operating procedure (TACSOP). (Appendix B provides additional guidance on integrating CCD into a unit's field TACSOP.) Generally, CCD is additive and synergistic with other defensive measures. CCD enhances unit survivability and increases the likelihood of mission success. A unit that is well trained in CCD operations more easily recognizes CCD as employed by an enemy, and this recognition enhances a unit's lethality.

## Evaluation

1-13. CCD training should be realistic and integrated with a unit's training evaluations. Employ the following techniques to enhance training evaluations:

- Have small-unit leaders evaluate their unit's CCD efforts from an enemy's viewpoint. How a position looks from a few meters away is probably of little importance. Evaluators should consider the following:
- Could an approaching enemy detect and place aimed fire on the position?
- From what distance can an enemy detect the position?
- Which CCD principle was ignored that allowed detection?
- Which CCD technique increased the possibility of detection?
- Use binoculars or night-vision or thermal devices, when possible, to show a unit how it would appear to an enemy.
- Use photographs and videotapes, if available, of a unit's deployments and positions as a method of self-evaluation.
- Incorporate ground-surveillance-radar (GSR) teams in training when possible. Let the troops know how GSR works and have them try to defeat it.
- Request aerial multispectral (visual, IR, radar) imagery of friendly unit positions. This imagery shows how positions appear to enemy aerial recon. Unit leaders should try to obtain copies of opposing forces (OPFOR) cockpit heads-up display (HUD) or videotapes, which are excellent assessment tools for determining a unit's detectability from an enemy's perspective. Another valuable

assessment tool is the overhead imagery of a unit's actions and positions. Overhead imagery is often difficult to obtain; but if a unit is participating in a large-scale exercise or deployment, the imagery probably exists and can be accessed through the unit's intelligence channels.

- Use OPFOR to make training more realistic. Supporting aviation in an OPFOR role also helps. When possible, allow the OPFOR to participate in the after-action review (AAR) following each mission. The unit should determine what factors enabled the OPFOR to locate, identify, and engage the unit and what the unit could have done to reduce its detectability.

## Other Considerations

1-14. Warfare often results in personnel losses from fratricide. Fratricide compels commanders to consider CCD's effect on unit recognition by friendly troops.

1-15. Army policy prescribes that camouflage aids be built into equipment and supplies as much as possible. Battle-dress uniforms (BDUs), paint, Lightweight Camouflage Screen Systems (LCSSs), and decoys help achieve effective camouflage. These aids are effective only if properly integrated into an overall CCD plan that uses natural materials and terrain. During training exercises, ensure that cutting vegetation or foliage does not adversely affect the natural environment (coordinate with local authorities). CCD aids should not interfere with the battlefield performance of soldiers or equipment or the installations that they are designed to protect. (See appendix C for more information on LCSSs.)

1-16. When employed correctly, expedient CCD countermeasures are often the most effective means of confusing an enemy. Along with the standard items and materials listed above, soldiers can use battlefield by-products, construction materials, and indigenous or locally procurable items to enhance unit CCD posture. For example, a simple building decoy can be constructed with two-by-fours and plywood. With the addition of a heat source, such as a small charcoal pit, the decoy becomes an apparently functional building. However, as with all CCD countermeasures, ensure that expedient treatments project the desired signatures to the enemy and do not actually increase the unit's vulnerability to detection. Expedient CCD countermeasures are also beneficial because the enemy has less time to study and become familiar with the selected countermeasures.

# CHAPTER 2 - THREAT

The enemy employs a variety of sensors to detect and identify US soldiers, equipment, and supporting installations. These sensors may be visual, near infrared (NIR), IR, ultraviolet (UV), acoustic, or multispectral/hyperspectral. They may be employed by dismounted soldiers or ground-, air-, or space-mounted platforms. Such platforms are often capable of supporting multiple sensors. Friendly troops rarely know the specific sensor systems or combination of systems that an enemy employs. When possible, friendly troops should protect against all known threat surveillance systems.

## Doctrine

2-1. Many threat forces were trained and equipped by the former Soviet Union. Its long-standing battlefield doctrine of maskirovka is a living legacy in many former Soviet-client states. Maskirovka incorporates all elements of CCD and tactical battlefield deception into a cohesive and effective philosophy. During the Gulf War, Iraq used maskirovka to effectively maintain its capability of surface-to-surface missiles (Scuds) in the face of persistent coalition-force attacks. Enemy forces that are trained in maskirovka possess a strong fundamental knowledge of CCD principles and techniques. Friendly forces must be very careful to conduct CCD operations so that a well-trained enemy will not easily recognize them.

2-2. Typical threat doctrine states that each battalion will continuously maintain two observation posts when in close contact with its enemy. An additional observation post is established when the battalion is in the defense or is preparing for an offense.

2-3. Patrolling is used extensively, but particularly during offensive operations. Patrols are used to detect the location of enemy indirect- and direct-fire weapons, gaps in formations, obstacles, and bypasses.

2-4. Enemy forces use raids to capture prisoners, documents, weapons, and equipment. A recon-in-force (usually by a reinforced company or battalion) is the most likely tactic when other methods of tactical recon have failed. A recon-in-force is often a deceptive tactic designed to simulate an offensive and cause friendly forces to reveal defensive positions.

## Organization

2-5. A typical enemy force conducts recon activities at all echelons. A troop recon is usually conducted by specially trained units. The following types of enemy units might have specific intelligence-collection missions:

- Troops. An enemy uses ordinary combat troops to perform recon. One company per battalion trains to conduct recon operations behind enemy lines.
- Motorized rifle and tank regiments. Each regiment has a recon company and a chemical recon platoon.
- Maneuver divisions. Divisions have a recon battalion, an engineer recon platoon, a chemical recon platoon, and a target-acquisition battery.

# Data Collection

2-6. An enemy collects information about United States (US) forces for two basic reasons—target acquisition and intelligence production. Enemy weapons systems often have sensors that locate and identify targets at long ranges in precise detail. Soldiers and units should take actions to hinder the enemy's target-acquisition process. These actions include all practical CCD operations expected to reduce the identification of soldiers, units, and facilities.

2-7. An enemy uses sensor systems to locate and identify large Army formations and headquarters (HQ) and to predict their future activities. Enemy detection of rear-area activities, such as logistics centers and communications nodes, may also reveal friendly intentions.

2-8. An enemy uses tactical recon to provide additional information on US forces' dispositions and the terrain in which they are going to operate. The enemy's tactical recon also attempts to identify targets for later attack by long-range artillery, rockets, aircraft, and ground forces.

# Sensor Systems

2-9. An enemy uses many different types of electronic surveillance equipment. Sensor systems are classified according to the part of the EM spectrum in which they operate. Figure 2-1 shows the EM spectrum and some typical enemy sensors operating within specific regions of the spectrum. An enemy uses detection sensors that operate in the active or passive mode:

- Active. Active sensors emit energy that reflects from targets and is recaptured by the emitting or other nearby sensor, indicating the presence of a target. Examples of active sensors are searchlights and radar.
- Passive. Passive sensors do not emit energy; they collect energy, which may indicate the presence of a target. Examples of passive sensors are the human eye, night-vision devices (NVDs), IR imaging devices, acoustic sensors, and photographic devices.

14

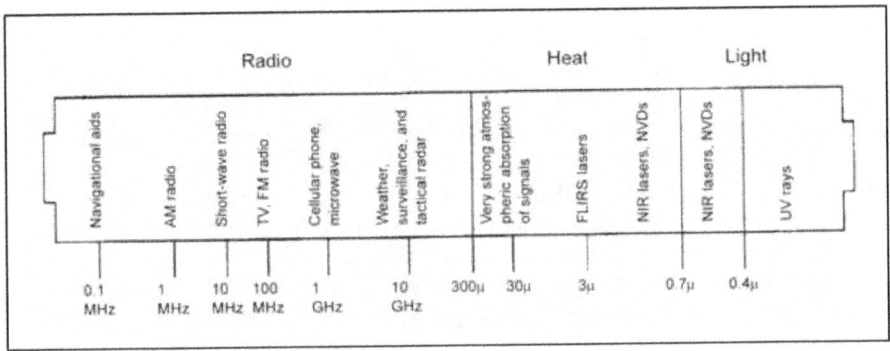

**Figure 2-1. EM spectrum**

## Visual

2-10. Visual sensors work in the parts of the EM spectrum that are visible to the human eye. Enemy soldiers' eyes are the principle sensors on a battlefield. They may be aided by binoculars, telescopic sights, and image intensifiers. Civilian populations, enemy agents, recon teams, and patrols are visual-sensor systems from the enemy's intelligence viewpoint. Three types of enemy visual sensors are—

- Image intensifiers. Image intensifiers are passive night-observation devices. They amplify the low-level light that is present on even the darkest nights. These devices are used for surveillance and as weapon sights on small arms and vehicles. Airborne platforms are also capable of supporting image intensifiers.
- Low-light television (LLTV). LLTV combines image intensification with television technology, and it is usually mounted on airborne platforms.
- Aerial recon, remote sensing, and imagery. Aerial photography, satellite imagery, and video imagery allow image analysts to record and study visual information. These analysts then produce target nomination lists that are, in effect, priority lists of targets in a given target scene. Since analysts often have to make subjective determinations of the identity and/or importance of a given target, the ranking of targets provides the defender with an opportunity to use CCD to impact an enemy's target-prioritization process. Video systems allow transmission of visual images to the ground while the manned aircraft, satellite, or unmanned aerial vehicle (UAV) is still in flight.

15

# Near Infrared

2-11. NIR sensors operate at a wavelength immediately above the visible light wavelength of the EM spectrum (figure 2-1). NIR energy reflects well from live vegetation but reflects better from dead vegetation and most man-made materials. NIR sensors, such as sights and periscopes, allow the human eye to detect targets based on differences in their reflection of NIR energy. NIR sensors are partially blocked by fog, mist, and smoke operations, although not as completely as visual sensors. An enemy's combat vehicles use active NIR sensors that employ searchlights, scopes, and sights; but these sensors are rapidly being replaced with image intensifiers and thermal gun sights.

# Infrared

2-12. IR sensors detect the contrasts in heat energy that targets radiate on the battlefield and display the contrasts as different colors or shades. Because longer wavelength IR radiation is more susceptible to atmospheric absorption than NIR radiation, IR sensors are less affected by typical concentrations of fog or conventional smoke.

2-13. Differences in thermal mass and surface properties (reflectivity) of man-made and natural materials result in target-to-background contrasts. These contrast levels change dramatically over a daily cycle. For example, operating vehicles and generators, heated buildings and tents, and soldiers are usually hotter than their background. Also, equipment exposed to direct sunlight appears hotter than most natural backgrounds. At night, however, equipment might appear cooler than its background if it is treated with special emissivity coatings. In other words, military equipment, particularly metallic equipment, generally heats up and cools off more quickly than its background.

2-14. Sophisticated, passive IR sensors (such as the Forward-Looking Infrared System [FLIRS]) can be mounted on aircraft. FLIRS sensors provide aircrews and enemy ground forces with real-time IR imagery that is displayed on video monitors.

2-15. Recon aircraft often employ special IR films to record temperature differences. Due to film processing, however, these systems are subject to time delays in obtaining the data. Newer versions of this sensor produce non-film-based images.

# Ultraviolet

2-16. The UV area is the part of the EM spectrum immediately below visible light. UV sensors are more important in snow-covered areas, because snow reflects UV energy well and most white paints and man-made objects do not reflect UV energy very well. Photographic intelligence systems with simple UV filters highlight military targets as dark areas against snow-covered backgrounds. These backgrounds require specially designed camouflage that provides a high UV reflectance.

## Radar

2-17. Radar uses high-frequency radio waves to penetrate atmospheric impediments such as fog, mist, and smoke. Radar works by transmitting a very strong burst of radio waves and then receiving and processing the reflected waves. In general, metal objects reflect radar waves well, while radar waves are either weakly reflected by or pass through most other objects. The shape and size of a metal object determine the strength of the reflected signal. A large, metal object generally reflects more signal than a small object. Therefore, large, metal objects can be detected from greater distances. The method by which the received radio wave is processed determines the type of radar. Radar systems commonly used against ground forces on the battlefield include—

- Moving-target indicators (MTIs). When an EM wave hits a moving target, the wave is reflected and changes frequency. The faster the target moves, the larger the changes in frequency. The simplest and most common battlefield radar detects this frequency change. Threat forces use MTIs for target acquisition. More sophisticated developmental radar systems, such as the Joint Surveillance Target Attack Radar System (JSTARS), use airborne surveillance platforms that downlink captured data to ground-station modules in near real time. Ground-based operators are then able to manipulate the data and gain heightened situational information, which is forwarded to command-and-control (C2) nodes to enhance tactical decision-making.
- Imaging radar. An imaging radar's receiver and processor are so sensitive that an image of the detected target is displayed on a scope. Imaging radar, such as side-looking airborne radar (SLAR), is generally used on airborne or space-borne platforms. Imaging radar typically does not provide the same resolution as the FLIRS and is less likely to be used for terminal target acquisition.
- Countermortar (CM) and counterbattery (CB) radar. CM and CB radar usually transmit two beams of energy that sweep above the horizon. An artillery or mortar round or a rocket passing through the beams reflects two signals that are received and plotted to determine the origin of the round.

## Acoustic

2-18. The three predominant types of acoustical detection systems are—

- Human ear. Every soldier, whether engaged in normal operations or at a listening post, is an acoustic sensor. However, visual confirmation is usually preferred.
- Flash-sound ranging. Flash-sound ranging is used against artillery. Light travels faster than sound, so enemy sound-ranging teams can determine the distance to a gun tube by accurately measuring the time between seeing a muzzle flash and hearing the sound. If the sound is detected by two or more teams, analysts plot the ranges using automated data-processing computers. The target is located where the plots intersect.
- Ground-based microphone array. Ground-based microphone-array systems allow listeners to record acoustic signatures and accurately triangulate their positions.

## Radio

2-19. Threat forces make a great effort to search for, detect, and locate the sources of US radio communications. They use various direction-finding techniques to locate opposing emitters. Once an emitter is detected, an enemy can take a number of actions, ranging from simply intercepting the transmissions to jamming or targeting the emitter for destruction.

## Multispectral & Hyperspectral

2-20. Recent advancements in sensor acquisition and information-processing technologies have fostered the advent of multispectral and hyperspectral sensors:

- Multispectral. Multispectral sensors typically scan a few broad-band channels within the EM spectrum. An example of a multispectral sensor might be one which coincidentally scans the visual and thermal IR portions of the EM spectrum. Such sensors allow an enemy to assess a cross section of EM wavelengths and acquire a target in one wavelength even though it might be effectively concealed in another.
- Hyperspectral. Hyperspectral sensors collect data across a continuous portion of the EM spectrum. These sensors scan many channels across a relatively narrow bandwidth and provide detailed information about target spatial and spectral patterns. Absorption and emission bands of given substances often occur within very narrow bandwidths. They allow high-resolution, hyperspectral sensors to distinguish the properties of the substances to a finer degree than an ordinary broadband sensor.

# CCD versus Threat Sensors

2-21. Target acquisition can be accomplished by a variety of sensors that operate throughout the EM spectrum. This poses a challenge in CCD planning and employment—determining which enemy sensor(s) that CCD operations should be designed to defeat. Unfortunately, no single answer is correct for all situations. Unit commanders without specific guidance from higher echelons assess their tactical situation and plan CCD operations accordingly. If intelligence data indicate that an enemy will use visual sensors for recon and target acquisition, then visual countermeasures must be employed. For IR or radar sensors, countermeasures that are effective in those spectra must be employed. If a multispectral or hyperspectral threat is anticipated, CCD operations are conducted to protect a unit in its most vulnerable EM bandwidths. Very few available camouflage materials or techniques provide complete broadband protection.

# CHAPTER 3 - FUNDAMENTALS

To remain a viable force on the battlefield, units must understand CCD fundamentals because they are essential to survivability. To design and place effective CCD, soldiers must constantly consider an enemy's point of view. (What will it see? What characteristics will its sensors detect?) Placing a low priority on CCD because of time constraints, minimal resources, or inconvenience could result in mission failure and unnecessary loss of life. (Appendix D contains more information on individual CCD.)

## Section I - Principles

### Avoiding Detection

3-1. The primary goal of CCD is to avoid enemy detection; however, this is not always feasible. In some cases, CCD may succeed by merely preventing an enemy from identifying a target. Simply avoiding identification is often sufficient to increase survivability. The following seven rules are critical when considering how to avoid detection or identification:

- Identify the enemy's detection capabilities.
- Avoid detection by the enemy's routine surveillance.
- Take countermeasures against the enemy's sensors.
- Employ realistic, CCD countermeasures.
- Minimize movement.
- Use decoys properly.
- Avoid predictable operational patterns.

### Identifying the Threat

3-2. Obtain as much information as possible about an enemy's surveillance capability. Intelligence preparation of the battlefield (IPB) should—

- Include the sensors that an enemy may use in a particular AO.
- Include information on the enemy's tactical employment of the sensors, if possible.
- Assess the impact of the enemy's surveillance potential on the target under consideration. This assessment varies with the relative positions of the sensor and the target on the battlefield, the role of the target, and the physical characteristics of the sensor and the target.

# Avoiding Detection by Routine Surveillance

3-3. Sophisticated sensors often have narrow fields of view. Furthermore, sensors can be very expensive and are unlikely to be deployed in such numbers as to enable coverage of the entire battlefield at all times. Sophisticated sensors are most likely to be deployed in those areas where an enemy suspects that friendly targets are deployed. The enemy may suspect that an area contains targets because of detection by less sophisticated, wider-coverage sensors or because of tactical analysis. Therefore, an important aspect of remaining undetected is to avoid detection by routine enemy surveillance.

3-4. Many sensors operate as well at night as they do during the day. Therefore, darkness does not provide effective protection from surveillance. Passive sensors are very difficult to detect, so assume that they are being used at night. Do not allow antidetection efforts to lapse during the hours of darkness. For example, conceal spoil while excavating a fighting position, even at night. Certain types of smoke will also defeat NVDs.

# Taking Countermeasures

3-5. In some cases, it might be appropriate to take action against identified enemy sensors. The ability to deploy countermeasures depends on a number of factors—the effective range of friendly weapons, the distance to enemy sensors, and the relative cost in resources versus the benefits of preventing the enemy's use of the sensor. An additional factor to consider is that the countermeasure itself may provide an enemy with an indication of friendly intentions.

# Employing Realistic CCD

3-6. The more closely a target resembles its background, the more difficult it is for an enemy to distinguish between the two. Adhering to this fundamental CCD principle requires awareness of the surroundings, proper CCD skills, and the ability to identify target EM signatures that enemy sensors will detect.

## Visual Sensors

3-7. The most plentiful, reliable, and timely enemy sensors are visual. Therefore, CCD techniques effective in the visual portion of the EM spectrum are extremely important. Something that cannot be seen is often difficult to detect, identify, and target. BDUs, standard camouflage screening paint patterns (SCSPPs), LCSS, and battlefield obscurants are effective CCD techniques against visual sensors. Full-coverage CCD helps avoid visual detection by the enemy. When time is short, apply CCD first to protect the target from the most likely direction of attack and then treat the remainder of the target as time allows.

21

## Near Infrared Sensors

3-8. NIR sights are effective at shorter ranges (typically 900 meters) than enemy main guns. While red filters help preserve night vision, they cannot prevent NIR from detecting light from long distances. Therefore, careful light discipline is an important countermeasure to NIR sensors and visual sensors (such as image intensifiers). BDUs, LCSS, battlefield obscurants, and SCSPPs are designed to help defeat NIR sensors.

## Infrared Sensors

3-9. Natural materials and terrain shield heat sources from IR sensors and break up the shape of cold and warm military targets viewed on IR sensors. Do not raise vehicle hoods to break windshield glare because this exposes a hot spot for IR detection. Even if the IR system is capable of locating a target, the target's actual identity can still be disguised. Avoid building unnecessary fires. Use vehicle heaters only when necessary. BDU dyes, LCSSs, IR-defeating obscurants, and chemical-resistant paints help break up IR signatures; but they will not defeat IR sensors.

## Ultraviolet Sensors

3-10. UV sensors are a significant threat in snow-covered areas. Winter paint patterns, the arctic LCSS, and terrain masking are critical means for defending against these sensors. Any kind of smoke will defeat UV sensors. Field-expedient countermeasures, such as constructing snow walls, also provide a means of defeating UV sensors.

## Radar

3-11. An enemy uses MTI, imaging, CM, and CB radars. Mission dictates the appropriate defense, while techniques depend on the equipment available.

### Moving-Target Indicator

3-12. MTI radar is a threat to ground forces near a battle area. Radar-reflecting metal on uniforms has been reduced, and Kevlar helmets and body armor are now radar-transparent. Plastic canteens are standard issue, and buttons and other nonmetal fasteners have replaced metal snaps on most field uniforms. A soldier wearing only the BDU cannot be detected until he is very close to MTI radar.

3-13. Soldiers still carry metal objects (ammunition, magazines, weapons) to accomplish their mission, and most radar can detect these items. Therefore, movement discipline is very important. Moving by covered routes (terrain masking) prevents radar detection. Slow, deliberate movements across areas exposed to radar coverage helps avoid detection by MTI radar.

3-14. Vehicles are large radar-reflecting targets, and a skilled MTI operator can even identify the type of vehicle. Moving vehicles can be detected by MTI radar from 20 kilometers, but travelling by covered routes helps protect against surveillance.

Imaging

3-15. Imaging radar is not a threat to individual soldiers. Concealing vehicles behind earth, masonry walls, or dense foliage effectively screens them from imaging radar. Light foliage may provide complete visual concealment; however, it is sometimes totally transparent to imaging radar. When properly deployed, the LCSS effectively scatters the beam of imaging radar. (See appendix C for more information.)

Countermortar & Counterbattery

3-16. Radar is subject to overload. It is very effective and accurate when tracking single rounds; however, it cannot accurately process data on multiple rounds (four or more) that are fired simultaneously. Chaff is also effective against CM and CB radar if it is placed near the radar.

## Acoustic Sensors

3-17. Noise discipline defeats detection by the human ear. Pyrotechnics or loudspeakers can screen noise, cover inherently noisy activities, and confuse sound interpretation.

3-18. It is possible to confuse an enemy by screening flashes or sounds. Explosives or pyrotechnics, fired a few hundred meters from a battery's position within a second of firing artillery, will effectively confuse sound-ranging teams. Coordinating fire with adjacent batteries (within two seconds) can also confuse enemy sound-ranging teams.

## Radio Sensors

3-19. The best way to prevent an enemy from locating radio transmitters is to minimize transmissions, protect transmissions from enemy interception, and practice good radiotelephone-operator (RATELO) procedures. Preplanning message traffic, transmitting as quickly as possible, and using alternate communication means whenever possible ensure that transmissions are minimized. To prevent the enemy from intercepting radio communications, change the radio frequencies and use low-power transmissions, terrain masking, or directional or short-range antennas.

# Minimizing Movement

3-20. Movement attracts the enemy's attention and produces a number of signatures (tracks, noise, hot spots, dust). In operations that inherently involve movement (such as offensive operations), plan, discipline, and manage movement so that signatures are reduced as much as possible. (See chapter 4 for information on disciplined movement techniques.)

# Using Decoys

3-21. Use decoys to confuse an enemy. The goal is to divert enemy resources into reporting or engaging false targets. An enemy who has mistakenly identified decoys as real targets is less inclined to search harder for the actual, well-hidden targets. The keys to convincing an enemy that it has found the real target are—

- Decoy fidelity (realism), which refers to how closely the multispectral decoy signature represents the target signature.
- Deployment location, which refers to whether or not a decoy is deployed so that the enemy will recognize it as typical for that target type. For example, a decoy tank is not properly located if it is placed in the middle of a lake.

3-22. A high-fidelity decoy in a plausible location often fools an enemy into believing that it has acquired the real target. Deploying low-fidelity decoys, however, carries an associated risk. If an enemy observes a decoy and immediately recognizes it as such, it will search harder for the real target since decoys are generally deployed in the same vicinity as the real targets. Plausible, high-fidelity decoys specifically designed to draw enemy fire away from real targets should be deployed to closely represent the multispectral signatures of the real targets. Properly deployed decoys have been proven in operational employment and experimental field tests to be among the most effective of all CCD techniques.

# Avoiding Operational Patterns

3-23. An enemy can often detect and identify different types of units or operations by analyzing the signature patterns that accompany their activities. For example, an offensive operation is usually preceded by the forward movement of engineer obstacle-reduction assets; petroleum, oils, and lubricants (POL); and ammunition. Such movements are very difficult to conceal; therefore, an alternative is to modify the pattern of resupply. An enemy will recognize repetitive use of the same CCD techniques.

# Applying Recognition Factors

3-24. To camouflage effectively, continually consider the threat's viewpoint. Prevent patterns in antidetection countermeasures by applying the following recognition factors to tactical situations. These factors describe a target's contrast with its background. If possible, collect multispectral imagery to determine which friendly target signatures are detectable to enemy sensors.

# Reflectance

3-25. Reflectance is the amount of energy returned from a target's surface as compared to the energy striking the surface. Reflectance is generally described in terms of the part of the EM spectrum in which the reflection occurs:

- Visual reflectance is characterized by the color of a target. Color contrast can be important, particularly at close ranges and in homogeneous background environments such as snow or desert terrain. The longer the range, the less important color becomes. At very long ranges, all colors tend to merge into a uniform tone. Also, the human eye cannot discriminate color in poor light.
- Temperature reflectance is the thermal energy reflected by a target (except when the thermal energy of a target is self-generated, as in the case of a hot engine). IR imaging sensors measure and detect differences in temperature-reflectance levels (known as thermal contrast).
- Radar-signal reflectance is the part of the incoming radio waves that is reflected by a target. Radar sensors detect differences in a target's reflected radar return and that of the background. Since metal is an efficient radio-wave reflector and metals are still an integral part of military equipment, radar return is an important reflectance factor.

# Shape

3-26. Natural background is random, and most military equipment has regular features with hard, angular lines. Even an erected camouflage net takes on a shape with straight-line edges or smooth curves between support points. An enemy can easily see silhouetted targets, and its sensors can detect targets against any background unless their shape is disguised or disrupted. Size, which is implicitly related to shape, can also distinguish a target from its background.

# Shadow

3-27. Shadow can be divided into two types:

- A cast shadow is a silhouette of an object projected against its background. It is the more familiar type and can be highly conspicuous. In desert environments, a shadow cast by a target can be more conspicuous than the target itself.
- A contained shadow is the dark pool that forms in a permanently shaded area. Examples are the shadows under the track guards of an armored fighting vehicle (AFV), inside a slit trench, inside an open cupola, or under a vehicle. Contained shadows show up

much darker than their surroundings and are easily detected by an enemy.

## Movement

3-28. Movement always attracts attention against a stationary background. Slow, regular movement is usually less obvious than fast, erratic movement.

## Noise

3-29. Noise and acoustic signatures produced by military activities and equipment are recognizable to the enemy.

## Texture

3-30. A rough surface appears darker than a smooth surface, even if both surfaces are the same color. For example, vehicle tracks change the texture of the ground by leaving clearly visible track marks. This is particularly true in undisturbed or homogeneous environments, such as a desert or virgin snow, where vehicle tracks are highly detectable. In extreme cases, the texture of glass or other very smooth surfaces causes a shine that acts as a beacon. Under normal conditions, very smooth surfaces stand out from the background. Therefore, eliminating shine must be a high priority in CCD.

## Patterns

3-31. Rows of vehicles and stacks of war materiel create equipment patterns that are easier to detect than random patterns of dispersed equipment. Equipment patterns should be managed to use the surroundings for vehicle and equipment dispersal. Equipment dispersal should not be implemented in such a way that it reduces a unit's ability to accomplish its mission.

3-32. Equipment paint patterns often differ considerably from background patterns. The critical relationships that determine the contrast between a piece of equipment and its background are the distance between the observer and the equipment and the distance between the equipment and its background. Since these distances usually vary, it is difficult to paint equipment with a pattern that always allows it to blend with its background. As such, no single pattern is prescribed for all situations. Field observations provide the best match between equipment and background.

3-33. The overall terrain pattern and the signatures produced by military activity on the terrain are important recognition factors. If a unit's presence is to remain unnoticed, it must match the signatures produced by stationary equipment, trucks, and other activities with the terrain pattern. Careful attention must also be given to vehicle tracks and their effect on the local terrain during unit ingress, occupation, and egress.

# Site Selection

3-34. Site selection is extremely important because the location of personnel and equipment can eliminate or reduce recognition factors. If a tank is positioned so that it faces probable enemy sensor locations, the thermal signature from its hot engine compartment is minimized. If a vehicle is positioned under foliage, the exhaust will disperse and cool as it rises, reducing its thermal signature and blending it more closely with the background. Placing equipment in defilade (dug-in) positions prevents detection by ground-mounted radar. The following factors govern site selection:

## Mission

3-35. The mission is the most important factor in site selection. A particular site may be excellent from a CCD standpoint, but the site is useful only if the mission is accomplished. If a site is so obvious that the enemy will acquire and engage a target before mission accomplishment, the site was poorly selected to begin with. Survivability is usually a part of most missions, so commanders must first evaluate the worthiness of a site with respect to mission accomplishment and then consider CCD.

## Dispersion

3-36. Dispersion requirements dictate the size of a site. A site has limited usefulness if it will not permit enough dispersal for survivability and effective operations.

## Terrain Patterns

3-37. Every type of terrain, even a flat desert, has a discernible pattern. Terrain features can blur or conceal the signatures of military activity. By using terrain features, CCD effectiveness can be enhanced without relying on additional materials. The primary factor to consider is whether using the site will disturb the terrain pattern enough to attract an enemy's attention. The goal is not to disturb the terrain pattern at all. Any change in an existing terrain pattern will indicate the presence of activity. Terrain patterns have distinctive characteristics that are necessary to preserve. The five general terrain patterns are—

- Agricultural. Agricultural terrain has a checkerboard pattern when viewed from aircraft. This is a result of the different types of crops and vegetation found on most farms.
- Urban. Urban terrain is characterized by uniform rows of housing with interwoven streets and interspersed trees and shrubs.
- Wooded. Woodlands are characterized by natural, irregular features, unlike the geometric patterns of agricultural and urban terrains.

27

- Barren. Barren terrain presents an uneven, irregular work of nature without the defined patterns of agricultural and urban areas. Desert environments are examples of barren terrain.
- Arctic. Arctic terrain is characterized by snow and ice coverage.

# CCD Discipline

3-38. CCD discipline is avoiding an activity that changes the appearance of an area or reveals the presence of military equipment. CCD discipline is a continuous necessity that applies to every soldier. If the prescribed visual and audio routines of CCD discipline are not observed, the entire CCD effort may fail. Vehicle tracks, spoil, and debris are the most common signs of military activity. Their presence can negate all efforts of proper placement and concealment.

3-39. CCD discipline denies an enemy the indications of a unit's location or activities by minimizing disturbances to a target area. To help maintain unit viability, a unit must integrate all available CCD means into a cohesive plan. CCD discipline involves regulating light, heat, noise, spoil, trash, and movement. Successful CCD discipline depends largely on the actions of individual soldiers. Some of these actions may not be easy on a soldier, but his failure to observe CCD discipline could defeat an entire unit's CCD efforts and possibly impact the unit's survivability and mission success.

3-40. TACSOPs prescribing CCD procedures aid in enforcing CCD discipline, and they should—

- List specific responsibilities for enforcing established CCD countermeasures and discipline.
- Detail procedures for individual and unit conduct in assembly areas (AAs) or other situations that may apply to the specific unit.

3-41. Units should have frequent CCD battle drills. CCD discipline is a continuous requirement that calls for strong leadership, which produces a disciplined CCD consciousness throughout the entire unit. Appendix B contains additional guidance for incorporating CCD into a unit TACSOP.

## Light & Heat

3-42. Light and heat discipline, though important at all times, is crucial at night. As long as visual observation remains a primary recon method, concealing light signatures remains an important CCD countermeasure. Lights that are not blacked out at night can be observed at great distances. For example, the human eye can detect camp fires from 8 kilometers and vehicle lights from 20 kilometers. Threat surveillance can also detect heat from engines, stoves, and heaters from great distances. When moving at night, vehicles in the forward combat area should use ground guides and blackout lights. When using heat sources is unavoidable, use terrain masking, exhaust baffling, and other techniques to minimize thermal signatures of fires and stoves.

## Noise

3-43. Individuals should avoid or minimize actions that produce noise. For example, muffle generators by using shields or terrain masking or place them in defilade positions. Communications personnel should operate their equipment at the lowest possible level that allows them to be heard and understood. Depending on the terrain and atmospheric conditions, noise can travel great distances and reveal a unit's position to an enemy.

## Spoil

3-44. The prompt and complete policing of debris and spoil is an essential CCD consideration. Proper spoil discipline removes a key signature of a unit's current or past presence in an area.

## Track

3-45. Vehicle tracks are clearly visible from the air, particularly in selected terrain. Therefore, track and movement discipline is essential. Use existing roads and tracks as much as possible. When using new paths, ensure that they fit into the existing terrain's pattern. Minimize, plan, and coordinate all movement; and take full advantage of cover and dead space.

# Section II – Techniques & Materials

## Techniques

3-46. CCD is an essential part of tactical operations. It must be integrated into METT-TC analyses and the IPB process at all echelons. CCD is a primary consideration when planning OPSEC. The skillful use of CCD techniques is necessary if a unit is to conceal itself and survive. A general knowledge of CCD methods and techniques also allows friendly troops to recognize CCD better when the enemy uses it. Table 3-1, lists the five general techniques of employing CCD—hiding, blending, disguising, disrupting, and decoying.

**Table 3-1. CCD techniques**

## Hiding

3-47. Hiding is screening a target from an enemy's sensors. The target is undetected because a barrier hides it from a sensor's view. Every effort should be made to hide all operations; this includes using conditions of limited visibility for movement and terrain masking. Examples of hiding include—

- Burying mines.
- Placing vehicles beneath tree canopies.
- Placing equipment in defilade positions.
- Covering vehicles and equipment with nets.
- Hiding roads and obstacles with linear screens.
- Using battlefield obscurants, such as smoke.

## Blending

3-48. Blending is trying to alter a target's appearance so that it becomes a part of the background. Generally, it is arranging or applying camouflage material on, over, and/or around a target to reduce its contrast with the background. Characteristics to consider when blending include the terrain patterns in the vicinity and the target's size, shape, texture, color, EM signature, and background.

## Disguising

3-49. Disguising is applying materials on a target to mislead the enemy as to its true identity. Disguising changes a target's appearance so that it resembles something of lesser or greater significance. For example, a missile launcher might be disguised to resemble a cargo truck or a large building might be disguised to resemble two small buildings.

## Disrupting

3-50. Disrupting is altering or eliminating regular patterns and target characteristics. Disrupting techniques include pattern painting, deploying camouflage nets over selected portions of a target, and using shape disrupters (such as camouflage sails) to eliminate regular target patterns.

## Decoying

3-51. Decoying is deploying a false or simulated target(s) within a target's scene or in a position where the enemy might conclude that it has found the correct target(s). Decoys generally draw fire away from real targets. Depending on their fidelity and deployment, decoys will greatly enhance survivability.

## Tests & Evaluation

3-52. Until recently, the effectiveness of CCD techniques had not been scientifically quantified. As such, CCD was not widely accepted in the US military as an effective means of increasing survivability. However, the Joint Camouflage, Concealment, and Deception (JCCD) Joint Test and Evaluation (JT&E) completed in 1995 measured the effectiveness of CCD against manned aerial attacks. It provided military services the basis for guidance on CCD-related issues. JCCD field tests were conducted in multiple target environments using a broad cross section of US attack aircraft flying against different classes of military targets. In controlled attack sorties, targets were attacked before and after employing CCD techniques.

3-53. The presence of CCD greatly reduced correct target attacks, particularly when decoys were employed as part of the CCD plan. Other JCCD findings included the following:

- CCD significantly increased aircrew aim-point error.
- CCD increased the target's probability of survival.
- Each CCD technique (hiding, blending, disguising, disrupting, and decoying) was effective to some degree in increasing the probability of survival.
- CCD was effective in all tested environments (desert, temperate, and subarctic).

# Natural Conditions

3-54. Properly using terrain and weather is a first priority when employing CCD. Cover provided by the terrain and by conditions of limited visibility is often enough to conceal units. The effective use of natural conditions minimizes the resources and the time devoted to CCD. The terrain's concealment properties are determined by the number and quality of natural screens, terrain patterns, and the type and size of targets.

## Forests

3-55. Forests generally provide the best type of natural screen against optical recon, especially if the crowns of the trees are wide enough to prevent aerial observation of the ground. Forests with undergrowth also hinder ground observation. Deciduous (leafing) forests are not as effective during the months when trees are bare, while coniferous (evergreen) forests preserve their concealment properties all year. When possible, unit movements should be made along roads and gaps that are covered by tree crowns. Shade should be used to conceal vehicles, equipment, and personnel from aerial observation.

## Open Terrain

3-56. Limited visibility is an especially important concealment tool when conducting operations in open terrain. The threat, however, will conduct recon with a combination of night-surveillance devices, radar, IR sensors, and terrain illumination. When crossing open terrain during limited visibility, supplement concealment with smoke.

## Dead Space

3-57. Units should not locate or move along the topographic crests of hills or other locations where they are silhouetted against the sky. They should use reverse

31

slopes of hills, ravines, embankments, and other terrain features as screens to avoid detection by ground-mounted sensors. IPB concealment and terrain overlays should identify areas of dead space. If overlays are not available, use the line-of-sight (LOS) method to identify areas of dead space.

## Weather

3-58. Conditions of limited visibility (fog, rain, snowfall) hamper recon by optical sensors. Dense fog is impervious to visible sensors and some thermal sensors, making many threat night-surveillance devices unusable. Dense fog and clouds are impenetrable to thermal sensors (IR). Rain, snow, and other types of precipitation hinder optical, thermal, and radar sensors.

## Smoke

3-59. Smoke is an effective CCD tool when used by itself or with other CCD techniques. It can change the dynamics of a battle by blocking or degrading the spectral bands that an enemy's target-acquisition and weapons systems use, including optical and thermal bands.

# Data Sources

3-60. Commanders must be able to evaluate natural conditions in their area to effectively direct unit concealment. They must know the terrain and weather conditions before mission execution. In addition to IPB terrain overlays, weather reports, and topographic maps, commanders should use aerial photographs, recon, and information gathered from local inhabitants to determine the terrain's natural concealment properties.

# Materials

3-61. Using natural conditions and materials is the first CCD priority, but using man-made materials can greatly enhance CCD efforts. Available materials include pattern-painted equipment, camouflage nets (LCSS), radar-absorbing paint (RAP), radar-absorbing material (RAM), false operating surfaces (FOSs), vegetation, expedient paint, decoys, and battlefield by-products (construction materials, dirt). (Appendix E lists man-made CCD materials that are available through the supply system.)

## Pattern Paint

3-62. Pattern-painted vehicles blend well with the background and can hide from optical sensors better than those painted a solid, subdued color. Pattern-painted equipment enhances antidetection by reducing shape, shadow, and color signatures. Improved paints also help avoid detection by reducing a target's reflectance levels in the visible and IR portions of the EM spectrum. The result is a vehicle or an item of equipment that blends better with its background when viewed by threat sensors.

While a patterned paint scheme is most effective in static positions, it also tends to disrupt aim points on a moving target. (See appendix E for a list of available paints.)

## Camouflage Nets

3-63. The LCSS is the standard Army camouflage net currently available, and it can be ordered through normal unit supply channels (see appendix E). The LCSS reduces a vehicle's visual and radar signatures. Stainless steel fibers in the LCSS material absorb some of the radar signal and reflect most of the remaining signal in all directions. The result is a small percentage of signal return to the radar for detection. The radar-scattering capabilities of the LCSS are effective only if there is at least 2 feet of space between the LCSS and the camouflaged equipment and if the LCSS completely covers the equipment. Do not place a radar-scattering net over a radar antenna because it interferes with transmission. The LCSS is also available in a radar-transparent model.

3-64. The three different LCSS color patterns are desert, woodland, and arctic. Each side of each LCSS has a slightly different pattern to allow for seasonal variations. The LCSS uses modular construction that allows the coverage of various sizes of equipment. (Appendix C discusses the required components and the instructions for assembling LCSS structures for different sizes of equipment.)

## Vegetation

3-65. Use branches and vines to temporarily conceal vehicles, equipment, and personnel. Attach vegetation to equipment with camouflage foliage brackets, spring clips, or expedient means (such as plastic tie-wraps). Use other foliage to complete the camouflage or to supplement natural-growing vegetation. Also use cut foliage to augment other artificial CCD materials, such as branches placed on an LCSS to break up its outline. Be careful when placing green vegetation since the underside of leaves presents a lighter tone in photographs. Replace cut foliage often because it wilts and changes color rapidly. During training exercises, ensure that cutting vegetation and foliage does not adversely affect the natural environment (coordinate with local authorities).

### Living Vegetation

3-66. Living vegetation can be obtained in most environments, and its color and texture make it a good blending agent. However, foliage requires careful maintenance to keep the material fresh and in good condition. If branches are not placed in their proper growing positions, they may reveal friendly positions to enemy observers. Cutting large amounts of branches can also reveal friendly positions, so cut all vegetation away from target areas.

3-67. Living vegetation presents a chlorophyll response at certain NIR wavelengths. As cut vegetation wilts, it loses color and its NIR-blending properties, which are related to the chlorophyll response. Replace cut vegetation regularly because over time it becomes a detection cue rather than an effective concealment technique.

3-68. Use dead vegetation (dried grass, hay, straw, branches) for texturing. It provides good blending qualities if the surrounding background vegetation is also dead. Dead vegetation is usually readily available and requires little maintenance; however, it is flammable. Due to the absence of chlorophyll response, dead vegetation offers little CCD against NIR sensors and hyperspectral sensors operating in the IR regions.

3-69. When selecting foliage for CCD, consider the following:

- Coniferous vegetation is preferred to deciduous vegetation since it maintains a valid chlorophyll response longer after being cut.
- Foliage cut during periods of high humidity (at night, during a rainstorm, or when there is fog or heavy dew) will wilt more slowly.
- Foliage with leaves that feel tough to the fingers and branches with large leaves are preferred because they stay fresher longer.
- Branches that grow in direct sunlight are tougher and will stay fresher longer.
- Branches that are free of disease and insects will not wilt as rapidly.

## Chlorophyll Response

3-70. Standard-issue camouflage materials (LCSS) are designed to exhibit an artificial chlorophyll response at selected NIR wavelengths. Nonstandard materials (sheets, tarps) are not likely to exhibit a chlorophyll response and will not blend well with standard CCD material or natural vegetation. Use nonstandard materials only as CCD treatments against visual threat sensors, not against NIR or hyperspectral threat sensors.

## Expedient Paint

*CAUTION: Expedient paint containing motor oil should be used with extreme caution.*

3-71. Use earth, sand, and gravel to change or add color, provide a coarse texture, simulate cleared spots or blast marks, and create shapes and shadows. Mud makes an excellent field expedient for toning down bright, shiny objects (glass, bayonets, watches). Add clay (in mud form) of various colors to crankcase oil to produce a field-expedient paint. Table 3-2 provides instructions on how to mix soil-based expedient paints. Use surface soils to mimic natural surface color and reflectivity.

| Paint Materials | Mixing | Color | Finish |
|---|---|---|---|
| Earth, GI soap, water, soot, paraffin | Mix soot with paraffin, add to solution of 8 gal water and 2 bars soap, and stir in earth. | Dark gray | Flat, lusterless |
| Oil, clay, water, gasoline, earth | Mix 2 gal water with 1 gal oil and ¼ to ½ gal clay, add earth, and thin with gasoline or water. | Depends on earth colors | Glossy on metal, otherwise dull |
| Oil, clay, GI soap, water, earth | Mix 1½ bars soap with 3 gal water, add 1 gal oil, stir in 1 gal clay, and add earth for color. | Depends on earth colors | Glossy on metal, otherwise dull |

*Note.* Use canned milk or powdered eggs to increase the binding properties of field-expedient paints.

**Table 3-2. Expedient paints**

## Radar-Absorbing Material

3-72. RAM was designed for placement on valuable military equipment. It absorbs radar signals that are transmitted in selected threat wave bands and reduces the perceived radar cross section (RCS) of the treated equipment. RAM is expensive relative to other CCD equipment and is not yet widely available. RAP offers the same RCS reduction benefits as RAM, and it is also expensive.

## Battlefield By-Products

3-73. Battlefield by-products (construction materials, dirt) can be used to formulate expedient CCD countermeasures. For example, use plywood and two-by-fours to erect expedient target decoys or use dirt to construct concealment berms.

## Decoys

3-74. Decoys are among the most effective of all CCD tools. The proper use of decoys provides alternate targets against which an enemy will expend ammunition, possibly revealing its position in the process. Decoys also enhance friendly survivability and deceive an enemy about the number and location of friendly weapons, troops, and equipment.

Employment Rationale

3-75. Decoys are used to attract an enemy's attention for a variety of tactical purposes. Their main use is to draw enemy fire away from high-value targets (HVTs). Decoys are generally expendable, and they—

- Can be elaborate or simple. Their design depends on several factors, such as the target to be decoyed, a unit's tactical situation, available resources, and the time available to a unit for CCD employment.
- Can be preconstructed or made from field-expedient materials. Except for selected types, preconstructed decoys are not widely available (see appendix E). A typical Army unit can construct effective, realistic decoys to replicate its key equipment and features through imaginative planning and a working knowledge of the EM signatures emitted by the unit.

3-76. Proper decoy employment serves a number of tactical purposes, to include—

- Increasing the survivability of key unit equipment and personnel.
- Deceiving the enemy about the strength, disposition, and intentions of friendly forces.
- Replacing friendly equipment removed from the forward line of own troops (FLOT).
- Drawing enemy fire, which reveals its positions.
- Encouraging the enemy to expend munitions on relatively low-value targets (decoys).

Employment Considerations

3-77. The two most important factors regarding decoy employment are location and fidelity (realism):

- **Location**. Logically placing decoys will greatly enhance their plausibility. Decoys are usually placed near enough to the real target to convince an enemy that it has found the target. However, a decoy must be far enough away to prevent collateral damage to the real target when the decoy draws enemy fire. Proper spacing between a decoy and a target depends on the size of the target, the expected enemy target-acquisition sensors, and the type of munitions directed against the target.
- **Fidelity**. Decoys must be constructed according to a friendly unit's SOP and must include target features that an enemy recognizes. The most effective decoys are those that closely resemble the real target in terms of EM signatures. Completely replicating the signatures of some targets, particularly large and complex targets, can be very difficult. Therefore, decoy construction should address the EM spectral region in which the real target is most vulnerable. The seven recognition factors that allow enemy sensors to detect a

target are conversely important for decoys. When evaluating a decoy's fidelity, it should be recognizable in the same ways as the real target, only more so. Try to make the decoy slightly more conspicuous than the real target.

# CHAPTER 4 – OFFENSIVE OPERATIONS

CCD countermeasures implemented during an offensive operation deceive the enemy or prevent it from discovering friendly locations, actions, and intentions. Successful CCD contributes to achieving surprise and reduces subsequent personnel and equipment losses.

## Preparations

4-1. The main CCD concern in preparing for offensive operations is to mask tactical unit deployment. While CCD is the primary means of masking these activities, deceptive operations frequently achieve the same goals.

### Signatures

4-2. Offensive operations create signatures that are detectable to an enemy. Analyzing these signatures may alert an enemy to the nature of an offensive operation (such as planning and location). Commanders at all levels should monitor operation signatures and strive to conceal them from enemy surveillance. These signatures include—

- Increasing scouting and recon activity.
- Preparing traffic routes.
- Moving supplies and ammunition forward.
- Breaching obstacles.
- Preparing and occupying AAs (engineer function).
- Preparing and occupying forward artillery positions.
- Increasing radio communications.

### Assembly Areas

4-3. Prepare AAs during limited visibility. They should then suppress the signatures that their preparations produced and remove any indications of their activities upon mission completion.

4-4. Designate AAs on terrain with natural screens and a developed network of roads and paths. Thick forests and small towns and villages often provide the best locations. If natural screens are unavailable, use spotty sectors of the terrain or previously occupied locations. Place equipment on spots of matching color, and take maximum advantage of artificial CCD materials.

4-5. Designate concealed routes for movement into and out of an area. Mask noise by practicing good noise discipline. For instance, armor movements can be muffled by the thunder of artillery fire, the noise of low-flying aircraft, or the transmission of sounds from broadcast sets.

4-6. Position vehicles to take full advantage of the terrain's natural concealment properties, and cover the vehicles with camouflage nets. Apply paint and cut vegetation to vehicles to enhance CCD at AAs and during battle. (When using vegetation for this type of CCD treatment, do not cut it from areas close to vehicles.) AAs are particularly vulnerable to aerial detection. Strictly enforce track, movement, and radio discipline. Remove tracks by covering or sweeping them with branches.

4-7. While at an AA, personnel should apply individual CCD. Applying stick paint and cut vegetation enhances CCD during all phases of an operation.

## Decoy

4-8. An enemy may interpret decoy construction as an effort to reinforce a defensive position. Laying false minefields and building bunkers and positions can conceal actual offensive preparations and give the enemy the impression that defenses are being improved. If necessary, conduct engineer preparation activities on a wide front so that the area and direction of the main attack are not revealed.

## Movement

4-9. Move troops, ammunition, supplies, and engineer breaching equipment forward at night or during limited visibility. Although an enemy's use of radar and IR aerial recon hinders operations at night, darkness remains a significant concealment tool. Select routes that take full advantage of the terrain's screening properties. Commanders must understand how to combine darkness and the terrain's concealing properties to conceal troop and supply movements.

4-10. When conducting a march, convoy commanders must strictly enforce blackout requirements and the order of march. Guidelines concerning lighting, march orders, and other requirements are usually published in SOPs or operation orders (OPORDs). Required lighting conditions vary depending on the type of movement (convoy versus single vehicle) and a unit's location (forward edge of the battle area [FEBA], division area, corps rear area). Inspect each vehicle's blackout devices for proper operation.

4-11. Enemy aerial recon usually focuses on open and barely passable route sectors. When on a march, vehicles should pass these types of sectors at the highest possible speeds. If prolonged delays result from encountering an unexpected obstacle, halt the column and disperse into the nearest natural screens. If a vehicle breaks down during a movement, push it off the road and conceal it.

4-12. When conducting a march during good visibility, consider movement by infiltration (single or small groups of vehicles released at different intervals).

Movement in stages, from one natural screen to the next, will further minimize possible detection. Use smoke screens at critical crossings and choke points.

4-13. During brief stops, quickly disperse vehicles under tree crowns or other concealment along the sides of the road. Strictly enforce CCD discipline. Watch for glare from vehicle windshields, headlights, or reflectors; and remedy the situation if it does occur. Try to control troop movement on the road or in other open areas. Conduct recon to select areas for long halts. The recon party should select areas that are large enough to allow sufficient CCD and dispersion. The quartering party should predetermine vehicle placement, develop a vehicle circulation plan, and guide vehicles into suitable and concealed locations. The first priority, however, is to move vehicles off the road as quickly as possible, even at the expense of initial dispersion. Use camouflage nets and natural vegetation to enhance concealment, and carefully conceal dug-in positions.

4-14. Traffic controllers have a crucial role in enforcing convoy CCD. Commanders should issue precise instructions for traffic controllers to stop passing vehicles and have the drivers correct the slightest violation of CCD discipline. Convoy commanders are responsible for the convoy's CCD discipline.

4-15. Pass through friendly obstacles at night, in fog, or under other conditions of poor visibility. Also use smoke screens because these conditions will not protect against many types of threat sensors. Lay smoke on a wide front, several times before actually executing the passage of lines. Doing this helps deceive an enemy about the time and place of an attack. Conceal lanes through obstacles from the enemy's view.

## Deceptive Operations

4-16. Conduct demonstrations and feints to confuse an enemy about the actual location of the main attack. Such deceptive operations are effective only if prior recon activities were conducted on a wide front, thereby preventing the enemy from pinpointing the likely main-attack area.

# Battle

4-17. Units should adapt to the terrain during a battle. Deploying behind natural vegetation, terrain features, or man-made structures maximizes concealment from enemy observation. Make optimum use of concealed routes, hollows, gullies, and other terrain features that are dead-space areas to enemy observation and firing positions. A trade-off, however, usually exists in terms of a slower rate of movement when using these types of routes.

4-18. Movement techniques emphasizing fire and maneuver help prevent enemy observation and targeting. Avoid dusty terrain because clouds of dust will alert an enemy to the presence of friendly units. However, if the enemy is aware of a unit's presence, dust can be an effective means of obscuring the unit's intentions in the same way as smoke. When natural cover and concealment are unavailable or impractical, the coordinated employment of smoke, suppressive fires, speed, and natural limited-visibility conditions minimize exposure and avoid enemy fire sacks. However, offensive operations under these conditions present unique training and C2 challenges.

4-19. Breaching operations require concealing the unit that is conducting the breach. Use conditions of poor visibility, and plan the use of smoke and suppressive fires to screen breaching operations.

4-20. Deliberate river crossings are uniquely difficult and potentially hazardous. Plan the coordinated use of terrain masking, smoke, decoys, and deceptive operations to ensure successful crossings.

# CHAPTER 5 – DEFENSIVE OPERATIONS

Successful defensive operations require strong emphasis on OPSEC. Proper OPSEC denies an enemy information about a friendly force's defensive preparations. Particularly important is the counter-recon battle, where defensive forces seek to blind an enemy by eliminating its recon forces. The winner of this preliminary battle is often the winner of the main battle. CCD, by virtue of its inherent role in counter-efforts, plays an important role in both battles.

## Preparations

5-1. The purpose of CCD during defensive preparations is to mask key or sensitive activities. Successful CCD of these activities leads to an enemy force that is blinded or deceived and therefore more easily influenced to attack where the defender wants (at the strengths of the defense). These key activities include—

- Preparing reserve and counterattack forces' locations.
- Preparing survivability positions and constructing obstacles (minefields, tank ditches).
- Establishing critical C2 nodes.

### Signatures

5-2. A number of signatures may indicate the intentions of friendly defensive preparations, and an enemy analyzes these signatures to determine the defensive plan. Specific signatures that could reveal defensive plans include—

- Working on survivability positions.
- Emplacing minefields and other obstacles.
- Moving different types of combat materiel into prepared positions.
- Preparing routes and facilities.
- Constructing strongpoints or hardened artillery positions.

### Counterattack & Reserve Forces

5-3. Due to the similarity of missions, the concerns for concealing counterattack and reserve forces are similar to those of maneuver forces engaged in offensive operations. Chapter 4 discusses considerations about AAs, troop and supply movements, passages of lines, and deception operations. This information is also useful as a guide when planning CCD for a counterattack.

# Planning

5-4. Proper planning is essential to avoid threat detection and prevent successful enemy analysis of the engineer efforts that are integral to defensive preparations. Engineer equipment creates significant signatures, so minimize its use to a level that is commensurate with available time and manpower. Disperse engineer equipment that is not required at the job site. Complete as much work as possible without using heavy equipment, and allow heavy equipment on site only when necessary. Engineers should minimize their time on site by conducting thorough, extensive planning and preparation. Additional signatures include—

- Supplies, personnel, and vehicles arriving to and departing from the unit area.
- Survivability positions being constructed.
- Smoke and heat emitting from kitchens, fires, or stoves.
- Communications facilities being operated.
- Educational and training exercises being conducted.

# Movement

5-5. Reserve forces should move along preplanned, concealed routes. They should also move and occupy selected locations at night or during other conditions of limited visibility. Quartering parties should preselect individual positions and guide vehicles and personnel to assigned locations. Light, noise, and track discipline are essential; but they are difficult to control during this phase. The quartering party should also develop a traffic-flow plan that minimizes vehicle and troop movement to and from the unit area.

5-6. Arriving units should immediately begin to conceal their positions. Commanders should detail the priorities for CCD in the OPORD, based on their assessment of which signatures present the greatest opportunity for threat detection.

# Assembly Areas

5-7. While AA CCD actions are similar to those of counterattack and reserve positions, the latter positions are more likely to be occupied longer. Therefore, CCD needs are more extensive and extended for counterattack and reserve forces. In fact, their CCD operations are often indistinguishable from those of support units.

5-8. Counterattack and reserve forces awaiting employment should capitalize on the time available to conduct rehearsals. While essential, these activities are prone to detection by an enemy's sensors so observe CCD discipline at all times and locations.

## Placement And Dispersal

5-9. Site selection is crucial when concealing engineer effort. Proper placement and dispersal of equipment and operations are essential. Use natural screens (terrain masking); however, urban areas often provide the best concealment for counterattack and reserve forces. (Chapter 7 discusses placement and dispersal in more detail.) When using forests as natural screens, carefully consider factors such as the height and density of vegetation, the amount and darkness of shadows cast by the screen, and the appropriateness of the particular screen for the season. The condition and quality of natural screens have a decisive effect on the capability to conceal units. Commanders should evaluate natural screens during engineer recon missions and conduct the missions on a timely, extensive basis.

5-10. The probability of detection increases considerably when survivability positions are prepared. Detection is easier due to the increased size of the targets to be concealed, the contrasting upturned soil, and the difficulty of concealing survivability effort. Despite these considerations, the enhanced protection afforded by survivability positions usually dictates their use. To minimize the probability of detection, employ a combination of natural screens and overhead nets to conceal construction sites.

## Camouflage Nets

5-11. Use camouflage nets (LCSS) to conceal vehicles, tents, shelters, and equipment. Use vegetation to further disrupt the outline of the target rather than completely hide it. Ensure that vegetation is not removed from a single location, because it could leave a signature for threat detection. Gather vegetation sparingly from as many remote areas as possible. This technique allows the immediate area to remain relatively undisturbed.

## Stoves & Fires

5-12. Strictly control the use of stoves and fires because they produce visual and thermal signatures detectable to threat sensors. If fires are necessary, permit them only during daylight hours and place them in dead ground or under dense foliage. Use nets and other expedient thermal screens to dissipate rising heat and reduce the fire's thermal signature.

## Communications

5-13. Monitor communications to prevent enemy intelligence teams from identifying unit locations.

## CCD Discipline

5-14. Strict CCD discipline allows the continued concealment of a unit's position. The longer a unit stays in one location, the harder it is for it to maintain

CCD discipline. Extended encampments require constant command attention to CCD discipline. The evacuation of an area also requires CCD discipline to ensure that evidence (trash, vehicle tracks) is not left for enemy detection.

# Survivability Positions & Obstacles

5-15. Survivability positions include fighting positions, protective positions (shelters), and trench-work connections. Such positions are usually constructed of earth and logs but may also be composed of man-made building materials such as concrete.

## Placement

5-16. Properly occupying positions and placing obstacles are critical CCD considerations. When possible, place obstacles and occupy positions out of the direct view of threat forces (such as a reverse-slope defense), at night, or under conditions of limited visibility.

## Backgrounds

5-17. Select backgrounds that do not silhouette positions and obstacles or provide color contrast. Use shadows to hinder an enemy's detection efforts. If possible, place positions and obstacles under overhead cover, trees, or bushes or in any other dark area of the terrain. This technique prevents the disruption of terrain lines and hinders aerial detection. CCD efforts, however, should not hinder the integration of obstacles with fires.

5-18. When using the terrain's natural concealment properties, avoid isolated features that draw the enemy's attention. Do not construct positions directly on or near other clearly defined terrain features (tree lines, hedge rows, hill crests). Offsetting positions into tree lines or below hill crests avoids silhouetting against the background and also counters enemy fire.

## Natural Materials

5-19. Use natural materials to supplement artificial materials. Before constructing positions and obstacles, remove and save natural materials (turf, leaves, humus) for use in restoring the terrain's natural appearance for deception purposes. During excavation, collect spoil in carrying devices for careful disposal. When preparing survivability positions and obstacles—

- Avoid disturbing the natural look of surroundings. Use camouflage nets and natural vegetation to further distort the outline of a position, to hide the bottom of an open position or trench, and to mask spoil used as a parapet. To further avoid detection, replace natural materials regularly or when they wilt or change color.

45

- Consider the effect of backblasts from rocket launchers, missile systems, and antitank weapons. Construct a concealed open space to the position's rear to accommodate backblasts. A backblast area should not contain material that will readily burn or generate large dust signatures.
- Use natural materials to help conceal machine-gun emplacements. Machine guns are priority targets, and concealing them is an essential combat task. Although CCD is important, placement is the primary factor in concealing machine guns.
- Place mortars in defilade positions. Proper placement, coupled with the use of artificial and natural CCD materials, provides the maximum possible concealment. Also consider removable overhead concealment.
- Use decoy positions and phony obstacles to draw enemy attention away from actual survivability positions and traces of obstacle preparation. Decoys serve the additional function of drawing enemy fire, allowing easier targeting of an enemy's weapons systems.

# Battle

5-20. CCD during the defensive battle is essentially the same as for the offensive battle. While a majority of the battle is normally fought from prepared, concealed positions, defensive forces still maneuver to prevent enemy breakthroughs or to counterattack. When maneuvering, units should—

- Adapt to the terrain.
- Make optimum use of concealed routes.
- Preselect and improve concealed routes to provide defensive forces with a maneuver advantage.
- Plan smoke operations to provide additional concealment for maneuvering forces.

# CHAPTER 6 – HIGH-VALUE TARGETS

The purpose of threat doctrine is for enemy forces to locate, target, and destroy deep targets, thereby degrading friendly capabilities while adding offensive momentum to attacking enemy forces. Enemy commanders focus their most sophisticated sensors in search of HVTs. By attacking these targets, enemy forces hope to deny adequate C2, combat support, or resupply operations to forward friendly forces throughout the battlespace. Therefore, properly employing CCD at key fixed installations, such as command posts (CPs) and Army aviation sites (AASs) is essential to survival on a battlefield. HVTs fall into two general classifications—fixed installations (section II) and relocatable units (section III). For information on camouflaging medical facilities, see appendix F.

## Section I – CCD Planning

### Plans

6-1. No single solution exists for enhancing the survivability of HVTs with CCD (except for large-area smoke screens). The characteristics of many such targets are unique and require the creative application of CCD principles and techniques. Therefore, the CCD planning process presented in this section is not intended to impose a regimen that must be followed at all costs. Rather, it suggests a logical sequence that has proven successful over time. In fact, the steps outlined below often lead to creative CCD solutions simply because they allow designers to consider the many options, benefits, and pitfalls of CCD employment. No CCD plan is wrong if it achieves the intended signature-management goals and does not impair mission accomplishment.

6-2. Each commander should develop his unit's CCD plan based on an awareness, if not a comprehensive assessment, of the detectable EM signatures emitted by HVTs under his command. He should evaluate these signatures by considering the enemy's expected RSTA capabilities (airborne and ground-based), knowledge of the target area, and weapons-on-target capability.

### Objective

6-3. A CCD plan increases target survivability within the limits of available resources. The design procedure must systematically determine which features of a given target are conspicuous, why those features are conspicuous, and how CCD principles and techniques can best eliminate or reduce target signatures. CCD should decrease the effectiveness of enemy attacks by interfering with its target-acquisition process, which in turn increases target survivability.

6-4. The steps outlined below provide guidance for designing CCD plans for HVTs. The detailed planning approach is applicable in any situation where CCD employment is necessary, but more so when the plans include HVTs.

Step 1. Identify the threat. Identify the principal threat sensors, weapon-delivery platforms, and likely directions of attack.

Step 2. Identify critical facilities. Identify critical HVTs. Include those that are critical from an operational standpoint and those that may provide reference points (cues) for an attack on more lucrative targets.

Step 3. Evaluate facilities. Once the critical HVTs are identified, focus efforts on identifying the target features that might be conspicuous to an enemy RSTA. Consider multispectral (visual, thermal, NIR, radar) signatures in this assessment. The seven recognition factors (chapter 3) are an excellent framework for conducting this assessment. Include a review of area maps, site plans, photographs, and aerial images of the target area.

Step 4. Quantify signatures. Quantify the multispectral signatures that are emitted by high-value facilities. Base the quantification on actual surveys of critical facilities, using facsimiles of threat sensors when possible. Specify the EM wavelengths in which targets are most vulnerable, and develop signature-management priorities.

Step 5. Establish CCD goals. Establish specific CCD goals for HVTs. These goals should indicate the signature reduction (or increase) desired and the resources available for CCD implementation. Base these goals on the results of steps 1 through 4. Change the CCD goals as the planning process develops and reiterate them accordingly.

Step 6. Select materials and techniques. Select CCD materials and techniques that best accomplish signature-management goals within logistical, maintenance, and resource constraints. Expedient, off-the-shelf materials and battlefield by-products are not identified in this manual, but they are always optional CCD materials.

Step 7. Organize the plan. Develop a CCD plan that matches goals with available materials, time and manpower constraints, and operational considerations. If the goals are unobtainable, repeat steps 5 and 6 until a manageable plan is developed.

Step 8. Execute the plan. Once a feasible CCD plan is developed, execute it. Store temporary or expedient materials inconspicuously. Conduct deployment training on a schedule that denies enemy intelligence teams the opportunity to identify the countermeasures or develop methods to defeat the CCD.

Step 9. Evaluate the CCD. The final step in the CCD planning process is to evaluate the deployed CCD materials and techniques. Important questions to ask in this evaluation include the following:

- Does CCD increase the survivability of HVTs?
- Does deployed CCD meet the signature-management goals outlined in the plan?
- Is deployed CCD operationally compatible with the treated target(s)?
- Are CCD materials and techniques maintainable within manpower and resource constraints?

# Section II – Fixed Installations

## Concept

6-5. Fixed installations (base camps, AASs, CPs, warehouses, roadways, pipelines, railways, and other lines-of-communication [LOC] facilities) provide scarce, nearly irreplaceable functional support to ground maneuver forces. The threat to these facilities is both ground-based and aerial. The CCD techniques for the two attack types do not necessarily change, but the defender must be aware of the overall implications of his CCD plan.

### Ground Attacks

6-6. Ground attacks against fixed installations (enemy offensives, terrorist attacks, and enemy special-force incursions) require constant operational awareness by the defenders. While most CCD techniques are conceptually designed to defend against an aerial attack, these same techniques can affect the target-acquisition capabilities of an enemy's ground forces to the benefit of the defender. SCSPP, LCSS, and natural vegetation provide CCD against a ground attack.

6-7. CCD discipline (light, noise, spoil) involves prudent operational procedures that friendly troops should observe in any tactical situation, particularly in the presence of hostile ground forces. (See chapter 5 for more information.)

### Aerial Attacks

6-8. Fixed installations are susceptible to aerial attacks because of their long residence time and immobility. However, fighter-bomber and helicopter aircrews face unique target-acquisition problems due to the relatively short time available to locate, identify, and lock onto targets. Fighter-bombers typically travel at high speeds, even during weapons delivery. This means attacking aircrews have limited search time once they reach the target area. Helicopters travel at slower speeds but generally encounter similar time-on-target limitations. Because of lower flying altitudes and slower speeds, helicopters are more vulnerable to ground defenses. In either case, proper CCD can increase aircrew search time, thereby reducing available time to identify, designate, and attack an HVT. The longer an aircrew is forced to search for a target in a defended area, the more vulnerable the aircraft becomes to counterattack.

## Enemy Intelligence

6-9. The location and configuration of most fixed installations are usually well known. CCD techniques that protect against sophisticated surveillance sensor systems, particularly satellite-based systems, can be costly in terms of manpower, materials, and time. Steps can be taken to reduce an enemy's detection of relocatable targets. Fixed installations are difficult to conceal from RSTA sensors due to the relatively long residence time of fixed installations versus relocatable targets. Unless the construction process for a given fixed installation was conducted secretly, defenders can safely assume that enemy RSTA sensors have previously detected and catalogued its location. Defenders can further assume that attacking forces have intelligence data leading them to the general area of the fixed installation. CCD design efforts, therefore, should focus on the multispectral defeat or impairment of the enemy's local target-acquisition process.

## CCD Techniques

6-10. Selected CCD techniques should capitalize on terrain features that are favorable to the defender and on the short time available to attacking aircrews for target acquisition. Use artificial and natural means to camouflage the installation. Where time and resources allow, deploy alternative targets (decoys) to draw the attention of the attacking aircrews away from the fixed installation.

6-11. Comprehensive CCD designs and techniques for fixed installations can be costly, yet field tests have shown that simple, expedient techniques can be effective. HVTs are usually supplied with artificial CCD materials. If they are not, soldiers increase the survivability of an installation by using CCD principles.

## Other Considerations

6-12. While standard CCD materials are designed to enhance fixed-installation survivability, they have practical limitations that are not easily overcome. Materials applied directly to a fixed installation may achieve the signature-management goals stated in the CCD plan. However, if other features of the target scene are not treated accordingly, the target may be well hidden but remain completely vulnerable.

6-13. For example, three weapons-storage-area (WSA) igloos are in a row. The middle igloo is treated with CCD materials while the other two are not. The middle igloo will still be vulnerable. The enemy knows that three igloos exist and will probably locate the middle one no matter how well the CCD plan is designed.

However, if all three igloos are treated with CCD materials and three decoy igloos are placed away from them, the treated igloos' survivability will increase.

6-14. Furthermore, if a man-made object (traffic surface) or a natural feature (tree line) is close to the igloos, attacking forces will use these cues to proceed to the target area even if all three igloos are treated with CCD materials. Remember, an HVT is part of an overall target scene and an attacker must interpret the scene. Do not make his task easy. CCD plans that treat only the target and ignore other cues (man-made or natural) within the target scene are insufficient.

# Command Posts

6-15. C2 systems provide military leaders with the capability to make timely decisions, communicate the decisions to subordinate units, and monitor the execution of the decisions. CPs contain vital C2 systems.

## Signatures

6-16. Since World War II, the size and complexity of CPs have increased dramatically. Their signatures have correspondingly increased from a physical and communications perspective (more types of antennas and transmission modes at a wider range of frequencies). As a result, the enemy can use several conspicuous signatures to detect and target CPs for attack. Therefore, CPs require excellent CCD to survive on the battlefield.

## Lines Of Communication

6-17. CPs are usually located near converging LOC, such as road or rail junctions, and often require new access and egress routes. Consider the following regarding CCD and CPs:

- Vehicle traffic. When evaluating EM signatures that CPs emit, consider concentrations of vehicles, signs of heavy traffic (characteristic wear and track marks), and air traffic. Park vehicles and aircraft a significant distance from CPs.
- Antennas. Antennas and their electronic emissions and numerous support towers are common to most CPs. Paint antennas and support equipment with nonconductive green, black, or brown paint if the surfaces are shiny. If tactically feasible, use remote antennas to reduce the vulnerability of the radio system to collateral damage.
- Security emplacements. Security measures (barbwire, barriers, security and dismount points, and other types of emplacements) can indicate CP operations. Barbwire exhibits a measurable RCS at radar frequencies. Ensure that barbwire and concertina wire follow natural terrain lines and are concealed as much as possible.

## Equipment

6-18. Power generators and other heat sources produce signatures that an enemy's surveillance and target-acquisition sensors can detect. Place heat-producing equipment and other thermal sources in defilade positions, within structures, or under natural cover. Heat diffusers, which tone down and vent vehicle exhaust away from threat direction, are an expedient means of thermal-signature reduction.

## Defensive Positions

6-19. Defensive positions (berms, revetments, fighting positions) for protection against direct- and indirect-fire attackers typically create scarred earth signatures and detectable patterns due to earth excavation.

## CCD

6-20. CCD improves OPSEC and increases survivability by minimizing the observable size and EM signatures of CPs. CP CCD requires recon, planning, discipline, security, and maintenance. Carefully controlled traffic plans decrease the possibility of disturbing natural cover and creating new, observable paths. Decoys are a highly effective means of confusing the enemy's target-acquisition process, particularly against airborne sensors. Against ground threats, the same general rules of CCD discipline apply; however, recon and heightened security patrols enhance CCD efforts against ground attack.

## Sites

6-21. CP sites, which could move every 24 hours, are still occupied for a longer period than AAs. CP site selection is crucial, therefore units should—

- Consider the needs of supporting an extended occupation while minimizing changes to natural terrain patterns. When constructing defensive positions, minimize earth scarring as much as possible. If scarred earth is unavoidable, cut vegetation, toned-down agents (paint), and camouflage nets help conceal scarred areas.
- Use existing LOC (roads, trails, streams). If a site requires construction of roads or paths, make maximum use of natural concealment and existing terrain. The fewer new lines required, the better the CP blends, leaving natural features relatively unchanged.
- Never locate a CP at a road junction. Road junctions are high-priority targets for enemy forces and are easily detectable.
- Locate a CP in an existing civilian structure, if possible, which simplifies hiding military activity. However, choose a structure in an area where a sufficient number of buildings with similar EM signatures can mask its location.

# Telecommunications Procedures

6-22. By strictly complying with proper radio, telephone, and digital communications procedures, the opportunities for an enemy to detect friendly telecommunications activities are minimized. Consider the following:

- Place antennas in locations using natural supports when possible (trees for dipoles). As a rule of thumb, place antennas a minimum of one wavelength away from surrounding structures or other antennas.

*Note. One wavelength is 40 meters (typically) for low frequencies and 1 meter for very high frequencies (VHFs).*

- Move antennas as often as possible within operational constraints.
- Use directional antennas when possible. If using non-directional antennas, employ proper terrain-masking techniques to defeat the threat's radio direction-finding efforts.
- Use existing telephone lines as much as possible. Newly laid wire is a readily observable signature that can reveal a CP's location. Communications wire and cable should follow natural terrain lines and be concealed in the best way possible.

## CCD Discipline

6-23. Maintain CCD discipline after occupying a site. Establish and use designated foot paths to, from, and within a CP's area. If a unit occupies a site for more than 24 hours, consider periodically rerouting foot paths to avoid detectable patterns. Conceal security and dismount points and other individual emplacements, and make paths to the CP inconspicuous. Enforce proper disposal procedures for trash and spoil. Rigidly enforce light and noise discipline. Enhance the realism of a decoy CP by making it appear operational. Allow CCD discipline to be lax in the decoy CP, thus making it a more conspicuous target than the real CP.

# Supply & Water Points

6-24. Supply and water points provide logistical support—the backbone of sustained combat operations. As these targets are relatively immobile and the object of an enemy's most sophisticated sensors, using CCD is one of the most effective means to improve their survivability.

## Operations

6-25. Many CCD methods associated with AAs and CPs also apply to supply and water points, but with additional requirements. Large amounts of equipment and supplies are quickly brought into tactical areas and delivered to supply points located as close to the FLOT as possible. Supplies must be unloaded and concealed quickly, while supply points remain open and accessible for distribution. Under these conditions, multiple supply points are generally easier to camouflage than single, large ones. Decoy supply and water points can also confuse a threat's targeting efforts.

## CCD

6-26. Take maximum advantage of natural cover and concealment. Configure logistics layouts to conform with the local ground pattern. Creativity can play a role in this effort. The following guidance enhances concealment of these operations:

- Avoid establishing regular (square or rectangular) perimeter shapes for an area.
- Select locations where concealed access and egress routes are already established and easily controlled.
- Use roads with existing overhead concealment if you need new access roads. Conceal access over short, open areas with overhead nets.
- Control movement into and out of the supply area.
- Mix and disperse supply-point stocks to the maximum extent possible. This not only avoids a pattern of stockpile shapes but also avoids easy destruction of one entire commodity.
- Space stocks irregularly (in length and depth) to avoid recognizable patterns. Stack supplies as low as possible to avoid shadows. Dig supplies in if resources allow. In digging operations, disperse the spoil so as not to produce large piles of earth.
- Cover stocks with nets and other materials that blend with background patterns and signatures. Flattops (large, horizontal CCD nets) are effective for concealing supply-point activities when resources allow their construction and when supply points are not too large. Dunnage from supply points provides excellent material for expedient decoys.

### Traffic Control

6-27. Ensure that vehicles cause minimal changes to the natural terrain as a result of movement into, within, and out of the area. Provide concealment and control of vehicles waiting to draw supplies. Rigidly practice and enforce CCD discipline and OPSEC. Debris control could be a problem and requires constant attention.

## Water Points

6-28. CCD for water points include the following additional considerations:

- Spillage. Water spillage can have positive and negative effects on a unit's CCD posture. Standing pools of water reflect light that is visible to observers. Pools can also act as forward scatterers of radar waves, resulting in conspicuous black-hole returns on radar screens. Therefore, minimize water spillage and provide adequate drainage for runoff. On the other hand, dispersed water can be used to reduce the thermal signatures of large, horizontal surfaces. However, use this technique sparingly and in such a way that pools do not form.
- Equipment. Use adequate natural and artificial concealment for personnel, storage tanks, and specialized pumping and purification equipment. Conceal water-point equipment to eliminate shine from damp surfaces. Conceal shine by placing canvas covers on bladders, using camouflage nets, and placing foliage on and around bladders. This also distorts the normal shape of the bladders.
- Scheduling. Enhance CCD discipline at water points by establishing and strictly enforcing a supply schedule for units. The lack of or violation of a supply schedule produces a concentration of waiting vehicles that is difficult to conceal.

## Army Aviation Sites

6-29. AASs are among the most important of all battlefield HVTs. AASs are typically comprised of several parts that make up the whole, including tactical assembly areas (TAAs), aviation maintenance areas (AMAs), forward operating bases (FOBs), and forward arming and refueling points (FARPs). The positioning of AAS elements with respect to each other is dynamic and often depends on the existing tactical situation. In the following discussion, an AAS will be defined as a TAA, an AMA, and a FARP collocated in the same area. While these elements are not always collocated, the CCD techniques for individual elements will not greatly differ based on positioning. Untreated AASs are detectable in most threat sensor wavelengths.

- **TAA**. A TAA is typically a parking area for helicopters. Helicopters are highly conspicuous targets because of their awkward shape, distinctive thermal signatures, and large RCS. An enemy expends a lot of time and energy attempting to locate TAAs. Once it finds them, the enemy aggressively directs offensive operations against them.
- **AMA**. The most conspicuous features of an AMA are the large transportable maintenance shelters. These shelters are highly

visible and indicate the presence of helicopters to an enemy. AMAs occupy large areas to allow for ground handling of aircraft. Traffic patterns around AMAs are also strong visual cues to the enemy. Maintenance assets, including aviation shop sets, have characteristically distinct multispectral cues.

- **FARP**. A FARP provides POL and ammunition support to AASs and other tactical units. A FARP consists of fuel bladders, heavy expanded mobility tactical trucks (HEMTTs), fueling apparatus, and bulk ammunition. Due to safety requirements, FARP elements are dispersed as much as possible within terrain and operational constraints. Each element is detectable with multispectral radar. In a FARP—
    - Fuel bladders contain petroleum liquids whose thermal mass is a strong IR cue relative to the background. Bladders are often bermed, which means that visible earth scarring is necessary to construct the berm.
    - Large HEMTTs are conspicuous in all wavelengths.
    - Fueling areas are generally arranged in such a way that the fueling apparatus (hoses, pumps) are arranged linearly in an open area for safe and easy access. The linear deployment of these hoses is a strong visual cue, and their dark color usually contrasts with the background. The dark hoses experience solar loading, and the POL liquids within the hoses can provide a thermal cue.

- **Equipment**. Palletized ammunition and support equipment accompany AASs. Such equipment is often stacked in regular, detectable patterns.

- **Aircraft**. Aircraft create large dust plumes when deployed to unpaved areas. Such plumes are distinct visual cues and indicate the presence of rotary aircraft to an enemy.
    - **Parked aircraft**. Camouflage nets, berms, stacked equipment, and revetments can effectively conceal parked aircraft. Vertical screens constructed from camouflage nets help conceal parked aircraft, particularly against ground-based threats. However, CCD techniques for rapid-response aircraft must not impair operational requirements, meaning that obtrusive, permanent CCD techniques are generally not an option. Also, foreign object damage (FOD) is a critical concern for all aviation assets. CCD for parked aircraft depends on the expected ground time between flights. The commanding officer must approve all aircraft CCD techniques before implementation.

- o **Aircraft refueling**. Aircraft refueling positions, particularly fuel hoses, should be dispersed and arrayed in a nonlinear configuration. The hoses can be concealed at periodic locations with cut vegetation or a light earth/sod covering to reduce visual and thermal signatures. Defensive positions. Constructing defensive positions can create detectable areas of scarred earth. CCD. AASs are extremely valuable targets; therefore, try to prevent their initial detection by an enemy.
- **Vehicles**. Large vehicles can be effectively concealed with camouflage nets. Also, properly placing these vehicles to use terrain features and indigenous vegetation increases their survivability. Expedient vehicle decoys provide an enemy with alternate targets, and proper CCD discipline is essential.
- **Dunnage**. Quickly conceal all dunnage (packing materials) to minimize the evidence of AASs.
- **Dust**. To avoid dust, park aircraft in grassy areas or where the earth is hard-packed. If such areas are unavailable, disperse water on the area to minimize dust plumes. However, water-soaked earth can also be an IR detection cue so use this option sparingly and, if possible, at night. Several chemical dust palliatives are available that provide excellent dust control for aviation areas.
- **Construction**. When constructing defensive positions, minimize disturbances to the surrounding area. Cover scarred earth with cut vegetation, camouflage nets, or toned-down agents.

# Section III – Relocatable Units

## Mobility & CCD

6-30. Examples of valuable relocatable units include TOCs, tactical-missile-defense (TMD) units (Patriot batteries), refuel-on-the-move (ROM) sites, and FARPs. These units are critical to offensive and defensive operations, and their protection should receive a high priority.

6-31. Mobility and CCD enhance the survivability of relocatable units. A CCD plan must include the techniques for units to deploy rapidly and conduct mobile operations continuously. The CCD techniques available to mobile units are basically the same as for fixed installations, and the principles of CCD still apply. However, the mission of relocatable units differs from that of fixed installations so CCD execution also differs.

6-32. Relocatable units spend from a few hours to several weeks in the same location, depending on their tactical situation. CCD techniques must be planned accordingly. If a unit is at a location for a few hours, it should employ expedient CCD techniques. If a unit is at a location for several days, it should employ robust CCD plans. The resources a unit expends on CCD execution must be weighed against the length of time that it remains in the same location. As CCD plans increase in complexity, subsequent assembly and teardown times also increase. Commanders must ensure that the unit's manpower and resources dedicated to CCD execution are equal to the tactical mobility requirements.

## Built-in Capabilities

6-33. CCD should be built into systems to the maximum extent possible. Supplemental CCD is usually necessary and should be designed to enhance the built-in CCD. Apply the same rules for avoiding detection and the same considerations regarding the seven recognition factors that are discussed in chapter 3. The CCD planning process outlined at the beginning of this chapter also applies.

# CHAPTER 7 – SPECIAL ENVIRONMENTS

The fundamentals of CCD do not change between environments. The seven rules for avoiding detection and the seven recognition factors that are listed in chapter 3 and the three CCD principles—preventing detection, improving survivability, and improving deception capabilities—still apply. However, the guidelines for their application change. Different environments require thoughtful, creative, and unique CCD techniques. This chapter discusses different CCD techniques that have proven effective in three special environments—desert, snow-covered areas, and urban terrain.

## Desert

7-1. The color of desert terrain varies from pink to blue, depending on the minerals in the soil and the time of the day. No color or combination of colors matches all deserts. Patches of uniform color in the desert are usually 10 times larger than those in wooded areas. These conditions have led to the development of a neutral, monotone tan as the best desert CCD paint color.

### Topography

7-2. Although desert terrain may appear featureless, it is not completely flat. In some ways, desert terrain resembles unplowed fields; barren, rocky areas; grasslands; and steppes.

### Shadows

7-3. The closer a target is to the ground, the smaller its shadow; and a small shadow is easier to conceal from aerial observation. The proper draping of CCD nets will alter or disrupt the regular, sharp-edged shadows of military targets and allow target shadows to appear more like natural shadows. When supplemented by artificial materials, natural shadows cast by folds of the ground can be used for CCD purposes. The best solution to the shadow problem in desert terrain is to dig in and use overhead concealment or cover. Otherwise, park vehicles in a way that minimizes their broadside exposure to the sun.

### Placement

7-4. Proper placement and shadow disruption remain effective techniques. Place assets in gullies, washes, wadis, and ravines to reduce their shadows and silhouettes and to take advantage of terrain masking. More dispersion is necessary in desert terrain than in wooded areas. Move assets as the sun changes position to keep equipment in shadows.

## Terrain Mottling

7-5. Use terrain mottling when the ground offers little opportunity for concealment. This technique involves scarring the earth with bulldozers, which creates darker areas on which to place equipment for better blending with the background. Ensure that the mottled areas are irregularly shaped and at least twice the size of the target you are concealing. Place the target off center in the mottled area and drape it with camouflage nets. When employing the scarring technique, dig two to three times as many scars as pieces of equipment being concealed. Doing this prevents the mere presence of mottled areas from giving away a unit's location.

## Movement Discipline

7-6. Movement discipline is especially important in the desert. Desert terrain is uniform and fragile, making it easily disturbed by vehicle tracks. Vehicle movement also produces dust and diesel plumes that are easily detectable in the desert. When movement is necessary, move along the shortest route and on the hardest ground. Shine is a particularly acute desert problem due to the long, uninterrupted hours of sunlight. To deal with this problem, remove all reflective surfaces or cover them with burlap. Use matte CCD paint or expedient paints (see table 3-2, page 3-12) to dull the gloss of a vehicle's finish. Shade optical devices (binoculars, gun sights) when using them.

## Noise & Light Discipline

7-7. Noise and light discipline is particularly important in desert terrain since sound and light can be detected at greater distances on clear desert nights. The techniques for reducing these signatures remain the same as for other environments. Be aware that thermal sensors, while not as effective during the day, have an ideal operating environment during cold desert nights. Starting all vehicle and equipment engines simultaneously is a technique that can be used to confuse enemy acoustical surveillance efforts.

# Snow-covered Areas

7-8. When the main background is white, apply white paint or whitewash over the permanent CCD paint pattern. The amount of painting should be based on the percentage of snow coverage on the ground:

- If the snow covers less than 15 percent of the background, do not change the CCD paint pattern.
- If the snow cover is 15 to 85 percent, substitute white for green in the CCD paint pattern.
- If the snow cover is more than 85 percent, paint the vehicles and equipment completely white.

## Placement

7-9. A blanket of snow often eliminates much of the ground pattern, causing natural textures and colors to disappear. Blending under these conditions is difficult. However, snow-covered terrain is rarely completely white so use the dark features of the landscape. Place equipment in roadways, in streambeds, under trees, under bushes, in shadows, and in ground folds. Standard BDUs and personal equipment contrast with the snow background, so use CCD to reduce these easily recognized signatures.

## Movement

7-10. Concealing tracks is a major problem in snow-covered environments. Movement should follow wind-swept drift lines, which cast shadows, as much as possible. Vehicle drivers should avoid sharp turns and follow existing track marks. Wipe out short lengths of track marks by trampling them with snowshoes or by brushing them out.

## Thermal Signatures

7-11. Snow-covered environments provide excellent conditions for a threat's thermal and UV sensors. Terrain masking is the best solution to counter both types of sensors. Use arctic LCSS and winter camouflage paint to provide UV blending, and use smoke to create near-whiteout conditions.

# Urban Terrain

7-12. Urbanization is reducing the amount of open, natural terrain throughout the world. Therefore, modern military units must be able to apply effective urban CCD. Many of the CCD techniques used in natural terrain are effective in urban areas.

## Planning

7-13. Planning for operations in urban areas presents unique difficulties. Tactical maps do not show man-made features in enough detail to support tactical operations. Therefore, they must be supplemented with aerial photographs and local city maps. Local government and military organizations are key sources of information that can support tactical and CCD operations. They can provide diagrams of underground facilities, large-scale city maps, and/or civil-defense or air-raid shelter locations.

## Selecting a Site

7-14. The physical characteristics of urban areas enhance CCD efforts. The dense physical structure of these areas generates clutter (an abundance of EM signatures in a given area) that increases the difficulty of identifying specific targets.

Urban clutter greatly reduces the effectiveness of a threat's surveillance sensors, particularly in the IR and radar wavelengths. Urban terrain, therefore, provides an excellent background for concealing CPs, reserves, combat-service-support (CSS) complexes, or combat forces. The inherent clutter in urban terrain generally makes visual cues the most important consideration in an urban CCD plan.

7-15. The regular pattern of urban terrain; the diverse colors and contrast; and the large, enclosed structures offer enhanced concealment opportunities. Established, hardened road surfaces effectively mask vehicle tracks. Depending on the nature of the operation, numerous civilian personnel and vehicles may be present and may serve as clutter. This confuses an enemy's ability to distinguish between military targets and the civilian population. Underground structures (sewers, subways) are excellent means of concealing movement and HVTs.

7-16. When augmented by artificial means, man-made structures provide symmetrical shapes that provide ready-made CCD. The CCD for fighting positions is especially important because of the reduced identification and engagement ranges (100 meters or less) typical of urban fighting. Limit or conceal movement and shine. These signatures provide the best opportunity for successful threat surveillance in urban terrain. Careful placement of equipment and fighting positions remains important to provide visual CCD and avoid detection by contrast (thermal sensors detecting personnel and equipment silhouetted against colder buildings or other large, flat surfaces).

## Establishing a Fighting Position

7-17. The fundamental CCD rule is to maintain the natural look of an area as much as possible. Buildings with large, thick walls and few narrow windows provide the best concealment. When selecting a position inside a building, soldiers should—

- Avoid lighted areas around windows.
- Stand in shadows when observing or firing weapons through windows.
- Select positions with covered and concealed access and egress routes (breaches in buildings, underground systems, trenches).
- Develop decoy positions to enhance CCD operations.

## Placing Vehicles

7-18. Hide vehicles in large structures, if possible, and use local materials to help blend vehicles with the background environment. Paint vehicles and equipment a solid, dull, dark color. If you cannot do this, use expedient paints to subdue the lighter, sand-colored portions of the SCSPP. When placing vehicles outdoors, use shadows for concealment. Move vehicles during limited visibility or screen them with smoke.

# APPENDIX A – METRIC CONVERSION CHART

This appendix complies with current Army directives which state that the metric system will be incorporated into all new publications. Table A-1 is a conversion chart.

| US Units | Multiplied By | Metric Units |
|---|---|---|
| Cubic feet | 0.0283 | Cubic meters |
| Feet | 0.3048 | Meters |
| Gallons | 3.7854 | Liters |
| Inches | 2.54 | Centimeters |
| Inches | 0.0254 | Meters |
| Inches | 25.4001 | Millimeters |
| Miles, statute | 1.6093 | Kilometers |
| Miles, statute | 0.9144 | Yards |
| Ounces | 28.349 | Grams |
| Pounds | 0.454 | Kilograms |
| Tons, short | 0.9072 | Tons, metric |
| Square feet | 0.093 | Square meters |
| Metric Units | Multiplied By | US Units |
| Centimeters | 0.3937 | Inches |
| Cubic meters | 35.3144 | Cubic feet |
| Cubic meters | 1.3079 | Cubic yards |
| Grams | 0.035 | Ounces |
| Kilograms | 2.205 | Pounds |
| Kilometers | 0.62137 | Miles, statute |
| Kilometers | 1,093.6 | Yards |
| Liters | 0.264 | Gallons |
| Meters | 3.2808 | Feet |
| Meters | 39.37 | Inches |
| Meters | 1.0936 | Yards |
| Millimeters | 0.03937 | Inches |
| Square meters | 10.764 | Square feet |
| Tons, metric | 2,204.6 | Pounds |

Table A-1. Metric conversion chart

# APPENDIX B – GUIDELINES FOR TACTICAL STANDING OPERATING PROCEDURES

TACSOPs are critical to battlefield success. All commanders should establish camouflage guidelines in their TACSOPs and ensure that their soldiers are familiar with them. TACSOPs provide guidelines that help reduce the time required to perform routine tasks. Commanders can achieve these ends by defining the responsibilities, identifying the expected tasks, and providing supervisors with a memory aid when planning or inspecting. TACSOPs, coupled with battle drills (appendix C), provide units with guidance on how to execute anticipated battlefield tasks. CCD employment is a task that should be routine for all units.

## Content

B-1. The following CCD considerations may be included in a unit TACSOP:

- A review of CCD fundamentals.
- Rules of unit CCD discipline.
- Memory aids for supervisors, which should include an inspection checklist (figure B-1, pages B-2 through B-4) and a chart of an enemy's sensor systems with possible countermeasures.
- Guidelines on CCD discipline to provide uniformity among all subunits.
- The different CCD postures.
- Procedures for blackout, the quartering party, unit movement, and the deployment area.
- Appropriate CCD postures in OPORDs for different missions.

## Commander's Responsibilities

B-2. Commanders must ensure that each soldier has the required quantities of serviceable BDUs and that these uniforms are properly maintained to protect their IR screening properties. Based on unit requirements, supply personnel forecast, request, and store adequate quantities of expendable CCD supplies (paint, makeup, repair kits). Commanders ensure that authorized quantities of CCD screens (LCSS) and support systems (to include repair kits and spare parts) are on hand and continually maintained in a clean, serviceable condition.

# Fratricide

B-3. Since warfare often results in the loss of life from fratricide, the unit TACSOP should include a way to reduce fratricide. Commanders should consider ways for friendly and allied units to identify each other on the battlefield. Fratricide compels commanders to consider the effect CCD and deception operations have on the necessity of being recognized by friendly troops.

**CCD Inspection Checklist**

1. Command Emphasis.
    a. The commander—
        (1) Establishes CCD goals.
        (2) Executes CCD plans.
        (3) Inspects frequently for CCD deficiencies.
        (4) Conducts follow-up inspection of CCD deficiencies.
        (5) Integrates CCD into training exercises.
    b. The unit—
        (1) Integrates CCD into its TACSOP.
        (2) Follows the TACSOP.
2. Discipline.
    a. The unit—
        (1) Observes noise discipline.
        (2) Observes light discipline with respect to smoking, fires, and lights.
        (3) Conceals highly visible equipment.
        (4) Covers shiny surfaces.
        (5) Keeps exposed activity to a minimum.
        (6) Uses cut vegetation properly.
        (7) Uses and conceals dismount points properly.
    b. Soldiers—
        (1) Wear the correct uniform.
        (2) Control litter and spoil.
3. Techniques. The unit—
    a. Places and disperses vehicles and equipment.
    b. Disperses the CP.
    c. Employs camouflage nets (LCSS).
    d. Uses (or minimizes) shadows.
    e. Minimizes movement.
    f. Hides operations and equipment.
    g. Blends operations and equipment with backgrounds.
    h. Employs pattern-painting techniques.
    i. Employs decoys.
    j. Integrates smoke operations with unit movement.

**Figure B-1. Sample CCD checklist**

k. Practices individual CCD on—

    (1) Helmet.

    (2) Face.

    (3) Weapon.

    (4) Other equipment.

l. Employs CCD on fighting positions by—

    (1) Eliminating or minimizing target silhouettes.

    (2) Practicing spoil control.

    (3) Eliminating or minimizing regular or geometric shapes and layouts.

    (4) Maintaining overhead concealment.

    (5) Practicing dust control.

m. Employs CCD on tactical vehicles by—

    (1) Minimizing and concealing track marks.

    (2) Minimizing or eliminating the shine on vehicles and equipment.

    (3) Reducing or using shadows to the unit's advantage.

    (4) Employing camouflage nets (LCSS).

    (5) Painting vehicles to match their surroundings.

    (6) Dispersing vehicles and equipment.

    (7) Concealing vehicles and supply routes.

    (8) Controlling litter and spoil.

    (9) Storing and concealing ammunition.

n. Employs CCD on AAs by—

    (1) Facilitating mission planning for access and egress concealment.

    (2) Marking guideposts for route junctions.

    (3) Ensuring that turn-ins are not widened by improper use.

    (4) Dispersing dismount, mess, and maintenance areas.

    (5) Dispersing the CP.

    (6) Maintaining CCD by—

        (a) Inspecting CCD frequently.

        (b) Controlling litter and garbage.

        (c) Observing blackout procedures.

**Figure B-1. Sample CCD checklist (continued)**

      (7)  Observing evacuation procedures by—

          (a)  Policing the area.

          (b)  Covering or eliminating tracks.

          (c)  Preventing traffic congestion.

          (d)  Concealing spoil.

o.   Employs CCD on the CP by—

      (1)  Ensuring that LOC are not converged.

      (2)  Dispersing vehicles.

      (3)  Ensuring that turn-ins are not widened through improper use.

      (4)  Ensuring that protective barriers follow terrain features.

      (5)  Concealing defensive weapons.

      (6)  Ensuring that existing poles are used for LOC.

      (7)  Digging in the CP (when in open areas).

      (8)  Maintaining camouflage nets (LCSS).

      (9)  Using civilian buildings properly by—

          (a)  Controlling access and egress.

          (b)  Observing blackout procedures.

          (c)  Avoiding obvious locations.

p.   Employs CCD on supply points by—

      (1)  Dispersing operations.

      (2)  Concealing access and egress routes.

      (3)  Using the track plan.

      (4)  Providing concealed loading areas.

      (5)  Developing and implementing a schedule for the units being serviced.

q.   Employs CCD on water points by—

      (1)  Concealing access and egress routes.

      (2)  Ensuring that the track plan is used.

      (3)  Controlling spillage.

      (4)  Controlling shine and reflections.

      (5)  Developing and implementing a schedule for the units being serviced.

**Figure B-1. Sample CCD checklist (continued)**

# APPENDIX C – CAMOUFLAGE REQUIREMENTS & PROCEDURES

This appendix provides information on the LCSS and describes how to erect it. Also included is a figure for determining the amount of modules needed to camouflage the various vehicles in the Army's inventory. This appendix also includes a sample battle drill that can be used to train soldiers.

## Lightweight Camouflage Screen System

C-1. The LCSS is a modular system consisting of a hexagon screen, a diamond-shaped screen, a support system, and a repair kit. You can join any number of screens to cover a designated target or area (figure C-1, page C-2). Use figure C-2, page C-3, to determine the number of modules needed for camouflaging a given area. Measure the vehicle or use table C-1, page C-4, to determine the vehicle's dimensions.

*Notes.*

> 1. *See appendix E for a list of LCSS national stock numbers (NSNs) and ordering information.*
> 2. *See TM 5-1080-200-13&P for more information on maintenance, erection, and characteristics of the LCSS.*

### Capabilities

C-2. The LCSS protects targets in four different ways. It—

- Casts patterned shadows that break up the characteristic outlines of a target.
- Scatters radar returns (except when radar-transparent nets are used).
- Traps target heat and allows it to disperse.
- Simulates color and shadow patterns that are commonly found in a particular region.

### Erecting Procedures

C-3. To erect camouflage nets effectively—

- Keep the net structure as small as possible.
- Maintain the net a minimum of 2 feet from the camouflaged target's surface. This prevents the net from assuming the same shape and thermal signature as the target it is meant to conceal.
- Ensure that the lines between support poles are gently sloped so that the net blends into its background. Sloping the net over the

target also minimizes sharp edges, which are more easily detectable to the human eye.

- Extend the net completely to the ground to prevent creating unnatural shadows that are easily detected. This ensures that the net effectively disrupts the target's shape and actually absorbs and scatters radar energy.
- Extend the net all the way around the target to ensure complete protection from enemy sensors.

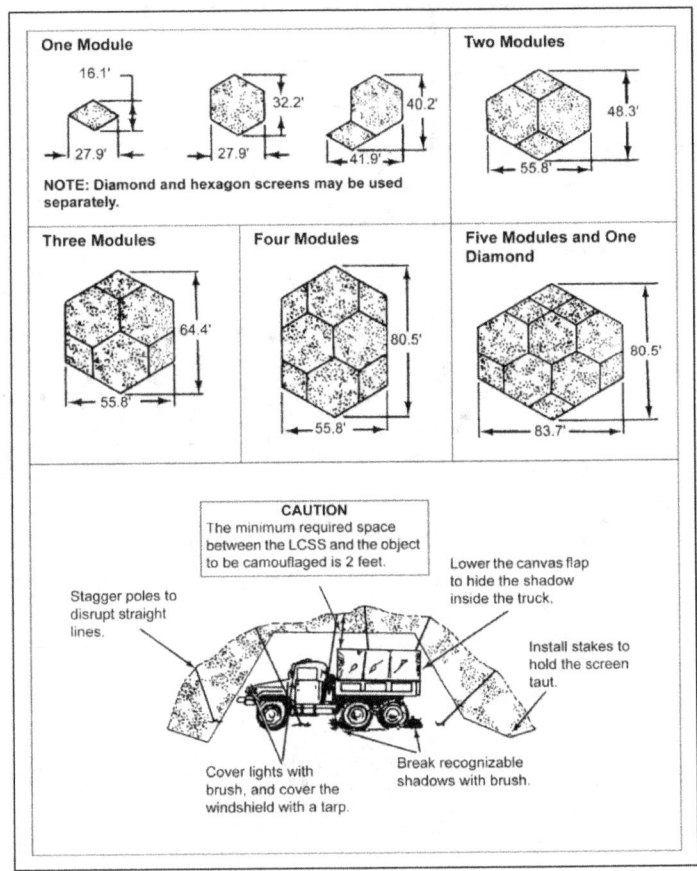

**Figure C-1. LCSS modular system**

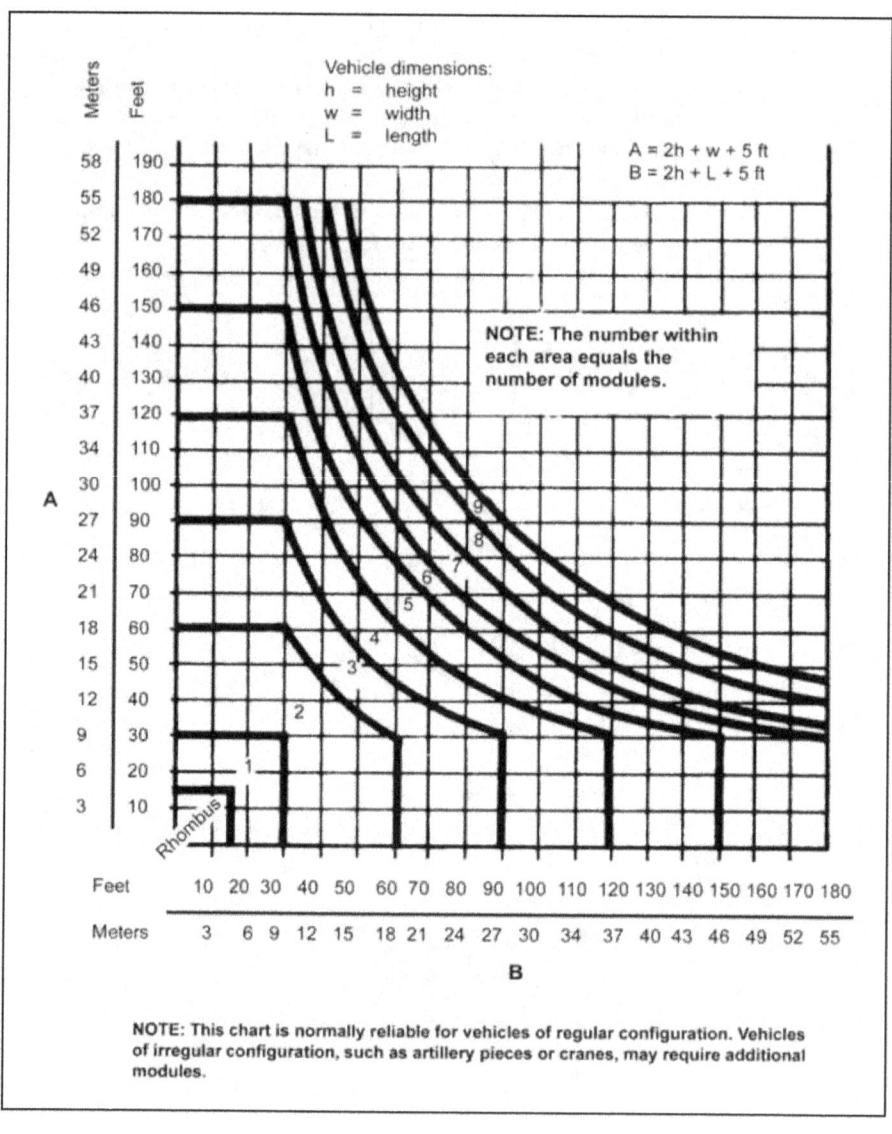

**Figure C-2. Module determination chart**

| Nomenclature | Height (feet) | Width (feet) | Length (feet) | No. of Modules |
|---|---|---|---|---|
| AVLB | 17 | 13 | 37 | 5 |
| C7 loader, scoop, 2½-ton, w/o cage | 9 | 9 | 25 | 2 |
| D7 dozer, with blade | 10 | 12 | 19 | 2 |
| M106A1 carrier, mortar, 107-mm | 7 | 10 | 16 | 2 |
| M109A3 howitzer, 155-mm (SP) | 11 | 12 | 30 | 3 |
| M113A2 carrier, personnel | 7 | 9 | 16 | 2 |
| M113A3 carrier, personnel | 7 | 9 | 19 | 2 |
| M125A1 carrier, mortar, 81-mm | 7 | 9 | 16 | 2 |
| M149 trailer, water, 400-gal | 6 | 7 | 7 | 1 |
| M172 trailer, low-bed, 25-ton | 6 | 10 | 35 | 2 |
| M1A1 tank, with mine roller | 10 | 12 | 40 | 3 |
| M1A1(2) tank, combat, 105- and 120-mm | 10 | 12 | 28 | 3 |
| M2 fighting vehicle, infantry | 10 | 11 | 22 | 2 |
| M2 TOW vehicle, improved | 11 | 9 | 15 | 2 |
| M3 fighting vehicle, cavalry | 10 | 11 | 22 | 2 |
| M35A2 truck, cargo, 2½-ton | 9 | 8 | 23 | 2 |
| M520 truck, cargo, 8-ton | 11 | 9 | 32 | 3 |
| M548 carrier, cargo, 6-ton | 10 | 9 | 21 | 2 |
| M54A2 truck, cargo, 5-ton | 10 | 8 | 26 | 2 |
| M553 truck, wrecker, 10-ton | 11 | 9 | 33 | 3 |
| M559 truck, fuel, 2,500-gal | 11 | 9 | 33 | 3 |
| M577A1 carrier, CP | 9 | 9 | 19 | 2 |
| M578 vehicle, recovery, light | 11 | 10 | 21 | 2 |
| M60A3 tank, combat, 105-mm | 11 | 12 | 27 | 3 |
| M713 truck, ambulance, ¼-ton | 7 | 6 | 12 | 2 |
| M728 vehicle, combat engineer | 11 | 12 | 29 | 3 |
| M792 truck, ambulance, 1½-ton | 8 | 7 | 19 | 2 |
| M816 truck, wrecker, 5-ton | 10 | 8 | 30 | 3 |
| M880 truck, cargo, 1¼-ton | 8 | 7 | 19 | 2 |
| M88A1 vehicle, recovery, medium | 10 | 11 | 27 | 3 |
| M9 vehicle, ACE | 9 | 13 | 21 | 2 |
| M920 truck, tractor, 20-ton | 12 | 11 | 27 | 3 |
| M930 truck, dump, 5-ton | 9 | 8 | 24 | 2 |
| M977 truck, cargo, HEMTT | 9 | 8 | 34 | 3 |
| M978 truck, tanker, HEMTT | 9 | 8 | 34 | 3 |
| M992 ammo carrier (FAAS-V) | 11 | 11 | 23 | 3 |
| M998, HMMWV, carrier, personnel | 6 | 7 | 15 | 2 |
| MLRS | 9 | 10 | 23 | 2 |
| MT250 crane, hydraulic, 25-ton | 10 | 8 | 45 | 3 |
| RT crane, boom, 20-ton | 14 | 11 | 44 | 4 |

**Table C-1. Vehicle dimensions**

73

# Supplemental Camouflage

C-4. Camouflage nets are often employed in conjunction with supplemental camouflage because nets alone do not make a target invisible to a threat's multispectral sensors. Use other CCD techniques to achieve effective concealment. Cover or remove all of the target's reflective surfaces (mirrors, windshields, lights). Also ensure that the target's shadow is disrupted or disguised. Use native vegetation, because placing a target in dense foliage provides natural concealment and a smoother transition between the edges of the camouflage net and the target's background. Cover exposed edges of the net with dirt or cut vegetation to enhance the transition.

# Vehicle Camouflage

C-5. Measure the vehicle or determine its dimensions from table C-1. Use the following equations and figure C-2, page C-3, to determine the number of modules needed to camouflage a vehicle.

Equation 1: $A = 2h + w + 5\ feet$

Equation 2: $B = 2h + L + 5\ feet$

where—

$h = height, in\ feet$

$w = width, in\ feet$

$L = length, in\ feet$

Step 1. Determine the vehicle's dimensions (measure or use table C-1). For the M2 fighting vehicle, the height is 10 feet, the width is 11 feet, and the length is 22 feet.

Step 2. Use the above equations and the measurements from Step 1 to determine the total dimensions.

$$A = 2(10) + 11 + 5 = 36\ feet$$
$$B = 2(10) + 22 + 5 = 47\ feet$$

Step 3. Determine the number of modules needed (use figure C-2). Since A equals 36 and B equals 47, two modules of camouflage are required to cover the M2 fighting vehicle.

# Training

C-6. Units should develop and practice battle drills that cover the requirements and procedures for erecting nets over assigned equipment. Table C-2, page C-6, shows a sample battle drill.

| |
|---|
| Standards:<br>• Complete camouflage net setup drills within 20 minutes.<br>• Complete camouflage net teardown drills within 15 minutes. |
| Personnel Required: Three crew members. |
| Equipment Required: Two modules or the following items:<br>• Nets, hexagonal, 2 each.<br>• Nets, diamond, 2 each.<br>• Pole sections, 24 each.<br>• Stakes, 36 each.<br>• Lanyards, 6 each.<br>• Spreaders, 12 each. |
| Stowage Location: The camouflage net is strapped to the right side of the trim vane. |
| Setup Drill:<br>• The gunner and the assistant gunner remove the camouflage net from the trim vane and place it on top of the M2.<br>• The driver removes poles and stakes from the bag and places them around the vehicle.<br>• The gunner and the assistant gunner remove the vehicle's antenna, position the net on top of the vehicle, and roll the net off the sides of the vehicle.<br>• The driver stakes the net around the vehicle.<br>• The driver and the assistant gunner assemble plies and spreaders and then erect the net.<br>• The gunner inspects the camouflage from a distance.<br>• The crew adjusts the camouflage as necessary. |
| Teardown Drill:<br>• The driver and the assistant gunner take down and disassemble plies and spreaders.<br>• The gunner and the assistant gunner unstake the net and roll it to the top of the M2.<br>• The gunner and the assistant gunner complete rolling the net on top of the vehicle and replace the vehicle's antenna.<br>• The driver stores the net on the trim vane.<br>• The gunner and the assistant gunner store poles, spreaders, and stakes on the trim vane. |
| *Notes.*<br>1. Preassemble the nets before placing them on the M2.<br>2. Supplement camouflage nets by properly placing vehicles and using natural vegetation. |

**Table C-2. Sample battle drill**

# APPENDIX D - INDIVIDUAL CAMOUFLAGE, CONCEALMENT, & DECOYS

Each soldier is responsible for camouflaging himself, his equipment, and his position. CCD reduces the probability of an enemy placing aimed fire on a soldier.

## Materials

D-1. Use natural and artificial materials for CCD. Natural CCD includes defilade, grass, bushes, trees, and shadows. Artificial CCD for soldiers includes BDUs, camouflage nets, skin paint, and natural materials removed from their original positions. To be effective, artificial CCD must blend with the natural background.

## Discipline

D-2. Noise, movement, and light discipline contribute to individual CCD:

- Noise discipline muffles and eliminates sounds made by soldiers and their equipment.
- Movement discipline minimizes movement within and between positions and limits movement to routes that cannot be readily observed by an enemy.
- Light discipline controls the use of lights at night. Avoid open fires, do not smoke tobacco in the open, and do not walk around with a lit flashlight.

## Dispersal

D-3. Dispersal is the deliberate deployment of soldiers and equipment over a wide area. It is a key individual survival technique. Dispersal creates a smaller target mass for enemy sensors and weapons systems. Therefore, it reduces casualties and losses in the event of an attack and also makes enemy detection efforts more difficult.

## Considerations

D-4. Every soldier should have a detailed understanding of the recognition factors described in chapter 3. While all of these factors remain important when applying individual CCD, the following factors are critical:

- **Movement.** Movement draws attention, whether it involves vehicles on the road or individuals walking around positions. The naked eye, IR, and radar sensors can detect movement. Minimize

76

movement while in the open and remember that darkness does not prevent observation by an enemy equipped with modern sensors. When movement is necessary, slow, smooth movement attracts less attention than quick, irregular movement.

- **Shape**. Use CCD materials to break up the shapes and shadows of positions and equipment. Stay in the shadows whenever possible, especially when moving, because shadows can visually mask objects. When conducting operations close to an enemy, disguise or distort helmet and body shapes with artificial CCD materials because an enemy can easily recognize them at close range.

- **Shine and light**. Shine can also attract attention. Pay particular attention to light reflecting from smooth or polished surfaces (mess kits, mirrors, eyeglasses, watches, windshields, starched uniforms). Plastic map cases, dust goggles worn on top of a helmet, and clear plastic garbage bags also reflect light. Cover these items or remove them from exposed areas. Vehicle headlights, taillights, and safety reflectors not only reflect light but also reflect laser energy used in weapon systems. Cover this equipment when the vehicle is not in operation. Red filters on vehicle dome lights and flashlights, while designed to protect a soldier's night vision, are extremely sensitive to detection by NVDs. A tank's red dome light, reflecting off the walls and out through the sight and vision blocks, can be seen with a starlight scope from 4 kilometers. Red-lensed flashlights and lit cigarettes and pipes are equally observable. To reduce the chances of detection, replace red filters with blue-green filters and practice strict light discipline. Use measures to prevent shine at night because moonlight and starlight can be reflected as easily as sunlight.

- **Color**. The contrast of skin, uniforms, and equipment with the background helps an enemy detect OPFOR. Individual CCD should blend with the surroundings; or at a minimum, objects must not contrast with the background. Ideally, blend colors with the background or hide objects with contrasting colors.

# Employment

D-5. Study nearby terrain and vegetation before applying CCD to soldiers, equipment, or the fighting position. During recon, analyze the terrain in lieu of the CCD considerations listed above and then choose CCD materials that best blend with the area. Change CCD as required when moving from one area to another.

# Skin

D-6. Exposed skin reflects light and may draw attention. Even very dark skin, because of natural oils, will reflect light. CCD paint sticks cover these oils and help blend skin with the background. Avoid using oils or insect repellent to soften the paint stick because doing so makes skin shiny and defeats the purpose of CCD paint. Soldiers applying CCD paint should work in pairs and help each other. Self-application may leave gaps, such as behind ears. Use the following technique:

- Paint high, shiny areas (forehead, cheekbones, nose, ears, chin) with a dark color.
- Paint low, shadow areas with a light color.
- Paint exposed skin (back of neck, arms, hands) with an irregular pattern.

D-7. When CCD paint sticks are unavailable, use field expedients such as burnt cork, bark, charcoal, lampblack, or mud. Mud contains bacteria, some of which is harmful and may cause disease or infection, so consider mud as the last resource for individual CCD field-expedient paint.

# Uniforms

D-8. BDUs have a CCD pattern but often require additional CCD, especially in operations occurring very close to the enemy. Attach leaves, grass, small branches, or pieces of LCSS to uniforms and helmets. These items help distort the shape of a soldier, and they blend with the natural background. BDUs provide visual and NIR CCD. Do not starch BDUs because starching counters the IR properties of the dyes. Replace excessively faded and worn BDUs because they lose their CCD effectiveness as they wear.

# Equipment

D-9. Inspect personal equipment to ensure that shiny items are covered or removed. Take corrective action on items that rattle or make other noises when moved or worn. Soldiers assigned equipment, such as vehicles or generators, should be knowledgeable of their appropriate camouflage techniques (see chapters 3, 4, and 5).

# Individual Fighting Positions

**Note.** *Review the procedures for camouflaging positions in chapter 5, which include considerations for camouflaging individual positions.*

D-10. While building a fighting position, camouflage it and carefully dispose of earth spoil. Remember that too much CCD material applied to a position can actually have a reverse effect and disclose the position to the enemy. Obtain CCD materials from a dispersed area to avoid drawing attention to the position by the stripped area around it.

D-11. Camouflage a position as it is being built. To avoid disclosing a fighting position, never—

- Leave shiny or light-colored objects exposed.
- Remove shirts while in the open.
- Use fires.
- Leave tracks or other signs of movement.
- Look up when aircraft fly overhead. (One of the most obvious features on aerial photographs is the upturned faces of soldiers.)

D-12. When CCD is complete, inspect the position from an enemy's viewpoint. Check CCD periodically to see that it stays natural-looking and conceals the position. When CCD materials become ineffective, change or improve them.

# APPENDIX E - STANDARD CAMOUFLAGE MATERIALS

Table E-1, lists standard camouflage items available to the soldier. Items on this list are ordered through normal unit-procurement channels:

A complete list of Department of Defense (DOD) stock materials is available from the Defense Logistics Service Center (DLSC), Battle Creek, Michigan, leon.cdidcodddengdoc@conus.army.mil .

A complete list of Army materials is available from the Army Materiel Command (AMC), Logistics Support Activity, Redstone Arsenal, Alabama, leon.cdidcodddengdoc@conus.army.mil.

| Item | NSN | Mil No. | Remarks |
|---|---|---|---|
| Camo enamel, black | 8010-00-111-8356 | NA | 5 gal |
| Camo enamel, black | 8010-00-111-8005 | NA | 1 gal |
| Camo enamel, sand | 8010-00-111-8336 | NA | 5 gal |
| Camo enamel, sand | 8010-00-111-7988 | NA | 1 gal |
| Camo screen, ultralite, asphalt/ concrete | 1080-01-338-4468 | PN88116169 | CVU-165/G |
| Camo screen, ultralite, green/tan | 1080-01-338-4471 | PN88116003 | CVU-166/G |
| Camo screen, ultralite, snow/partial snow | 1080-01-338-4469 | PN88116170 | CVU-164/G |
| Camo support set, ultralite (A-frame) | 1080-01-338-4472 | PN88116154 | MTU-96/G |
| Connector plug, w/o gen-test | 5935-01-050-6586 | MS3456W16S-1P | Use 5935-00-431-4935 |
| Connector, receptacle, electrical CCK-77/E | 1370-01-171-1336 | 293E663P404 | 1.4G class/div, 49 ea |
| Control, remote smoke gen, MXK-856/E32 | 1080-01-338-7051 | PN88115510 | For SG-18-02 |
| Decoy target, bailey bridge | 1080-00-650-1098 | MIL-D-52165 | None |
| Decoy target, how, 105-mm | 1080-00-570-6519 | MIL-D-52165B | PN EB 306D4904-IT08 |
| Decoy units, inflating, radar, AN/SLQ-49 | 5865-01-266-3840 | MRIIRVIN820/821 | Passive radar freq respondent |
| Decoy, aircraft, ground (F-16) | 1080-01-301-8273 | PN160002 | Only 25 produced |
| Decoy, close combat, M1A1 tank | 1080-01-242-7251 | PN13277E9830 | None |
| Decoy, close combat, M60A3 tank | 1080-01-242-7250 | PN3228E1979 | None |
| Decoy, runway (FOS) | 1080-01-338-5201 | PN88116100 | 50 x 1,000 ft |
| Diesel fuel, DF-1 | 9140-00-286-5288 | VV-F-800D | Smoke/obsc-alt |
| Diesel fuel, DF-2 | 9140-00-286-5296 | VV-F-800D | Smoke/obsc-alt |
| Diesel fuel, DF-2 | 9140-00-286-5297 | VV-F-800D | Smoke/obsc-alt |
| Drum, S&S, 55-gal | 8110-00-292-9783 | NA | 18-gauge steel, painted |
| Drum, S&S, 55-gal | 8110-00-597-2353 | NA | 16-gauge steel, painted |

**Table E-1. Camouflage items**

| Item | NSN | Mil No. | Remarks |
|---|---|---|---|
| Explosive, airburst projectile launch atk | 1055-01-175-4002 | PN102575 | Smoky flak, LMK-25 |
| Federal standard colors 595-B | 7690-01-162-2210 | NA | 2-ft x 10-in fan deck of color |
| Gen set, smoke, mech, M157 | 1040-01-206-0147 | PN31-15-255 | None |
| Gen, signal radio freq | 6625-00-937-4029 | NA | SM-422/GRC |
| Gen, smoke, mech, A/E32U-13 | 1040-01-338-8839 | PN88115460 | SG-18-02 |
| Gen, smoke, mech, M3A | 1040-00-587-3618 | MILSTD604 | None |
| Gen, smoke, mech, M3A4 | 1040-01-143-9506 | MILSTD604 | PN E31-15-2000 |
| Indiv camo cover, 3-color woodland | 8415-01-280-3098 | MIL-C-44358 | 8 oz, 5- x 8-ft coverage |
| Indiv camo cover, 6-color desert | 8415-01-280-5234 | MIL-C-44358 | 8 oz, 5- x 8-ft coverage |
| Indiv camo cover, snow | 8415-01-282-3160 | MIL-C-44358 | 8 oz, 5- x 8-ft coverage |
| Launcher rckt, 1-bay launcher, LMU-23E | 1055-01-131-7857 | PN1335AS380 | Smoky SAM |
| Launcher rckt, 4-bay launcher, OMU-24E | 1055-01-144-0864 | PN1335AS700 | Smoky SAM |
| LCSS support set, desert | 1080-00-623-7295 | MIL-C-52765 | Can use 1080-01-253-0522 |
| LCSS support set, snow | 1080-00-556-4954 | MIL-C-52765 | Same as 1080-01-179-6024 |
| LCSS support set, woodland | 1080-00-108-1173 | MIL-C-52765 | Same as 1080-01-179-6025 |
| LCSS support set, woodland | 1080-00-108-1173 | MIL-C-52765 | Plastic poles |
| LCSS, desert, radar-scattering | 1080-00-103-1211 | MIL-C-52771 | Can use 1080-01-266-1828 |
| LCSS, desert, radar-scattering | 1080-01-266-1825 | PN13228E5930 | Can use 1080-01-266-1828 |
| LCSS, desert, radar-scattering | 1080-01-266-1828 | PN13228E5933 | Use 1080-01-266-1825 first |
| LCSS, desert, radar-transparent | 1080-00-103-1217 | MIL-C52765 | PN13226E1357 |
| LCSS, snow, radar-scattering | 1080-00-103-1233 | MIL-C-52765 | Can use 1080-01-266-1826 |
| LCSS, snow, radar-scattering | 1080-00-103-1234 | MIL-C-52765 | PN13226E1355 |
| LCSS, snow, radar-scattering | 1080-01-266-1823 | PN13228E5928 | Can use 1080-01-266-1826 |
| LCSS, snow, radar-scattering | 1080-01-266-1826 | PN13228E5931 | Can use 1080-00-103-1233 |
| LCSS, woodland, radar-scattering | 1080-00-103-1246 | MIL-C-53004 | Can use 1080-01-266-1827 |
| LCSS, woodland, radar-scattering | 1080-00-103-1322 | MIL-C-53004 | PN13226E1356 |
| LCSS, woodland, radar-scattering | 1080-01-266-1824 | PN13228E5929 | Can use 1080-01-266-1827 |
| LCSS, woodland, radar-scattering | 1080-01-266-1827 | PN13228E5932 | Use 1080-01-266-1824 first |
| Lead acid btry, 24V, BB-297U | 6140-00-059-3528 | MS75047-1 | For SG 18-02 w/o gen |
| Mounting kit, smoke gen, M284 | 1040-01-249-0272 | PN31-14-2680 | For M157 gen |
| Net, multipurpose, olive-green mesh | 8465-00-889-3771 | MIL-N-43181 | 108- x 60-in coverage |
| Paint, temp, tan | 8010-01-326-8078 | MIL-P-52905 | Fed-std-595B 33446 |
| Paint, temp, tan | 8010-01-326-8079 | MIL-P-52905 | Fed-std-595B 33446 |
| Paint, temp, white | 8010-01-129-5444 | MIL-P-52905 | None |

**Table E-1. Camouflage items**

81

| Item | NSN | Mil No. | Remarks |
|------|-----|---------|---------|
| Pump inflating, manual, smoky flak | 4320-00-822-9036 | XX-P-746 | Need 1 ea TO 11A-1-46 |
| Reflector, radar, Coast Guard buoy marker | 2050-01-225-2779 | 120768 | 1 cu ft, 10-lb, aluminum |
| Simulator, atomic explosion, M142 | 1370-00-474-0270 | MIL-S-46528(1) | PM8864243 |
| Simulator, projectile airburst, PJU-7/E | 1370-01-180-5856 | PN102549 | 1.1G class/div, 48 ea |
| Simulator, projectile airburst, PJU-7A/E | 1370-01-279-9505 | PN8387310 | 1.3G class/div, 48 ea |
| Smoke pot, 30-lb, HC, M5 | 1365-00-598-5207 | MIL-S-13183 | PH E36-1-18, ±17 min |
| Smoke pot, floating, HC | 1365-00-939-6599 | MIL-S-51235 | w/M208/M209 fuse |
| Smoke pot, floating, HC, M4A2 | 1365-00-598-5220 | MIL-S-51235B | w/M207a fuse, ±12 min |
| Smokey SAM rocket, GTR-18A | 1340-01-130-6282 | DL1335AS100 | Firing cartridge and rocket |
| Support poles, camo net, ultralite | 1080-01-338-4470 | PN88116153 | MTU-99/G, 2 poles/battens |
| Tool, special purpose, smoky flak | 5120-01-176-2188 | PN103320 | Need 1 ea |
| Trailer, ground-handling, MHU-141/M | 1740-01-031-5868 | MIL-BK-300 | 5,500-lb cap, for SG-18-02 |
| Valve adapter assy, smoky flak | 1055-01-216-4803 | PN8523971-10 | Need 1 each |
| Valve, pneumatic tank, smoky flak | 4820-00-427-5047 | GV500RK2 | Need 1 ea |
| Wrench, bung | 5120-00-045-5055 | Cage #07227 | 2- x 3/4-in plugs |

**Table E-1. Camouflage items**

# APPENDIX F – THE GENEVA EMBLEM & CAMOUFLAGE OF MEDICAL FACILITIES

*This appendix implements STANAG 2931.*

STANAG 2931 covers procedures for using the Geneva emblem and camouflaging medical facilities. This STANAG requires signatories to display the Geneva emblem (red cross) on medical facilities to help identify and protect the sick and wounded. All signatories, however, are allowed to display the Geneva emblem according to their national regulations and procedures. STANAG 2931 also defines medical facilities as medical units, medical vehicles, and medical aircraft on the ground. A tactical commander may order the camouflage of medical facilities, including the Geneva emblem, when the failure to do so will endanger or compromise tactical operations. Such an order is considered temporary and must be rescinded as soon as the tactical situation permits. The camouflage of large, fixed medical facilities is not envisaged under the guidelines of STANAG 2931.

# GLOSSARY

Acronym/Term Definition

| | |
|---|---|
| AA | assembly area |
| AAR | after-action review |
| AAS | Army aviation site |
| ACE | armored combat earthmover, M9 |
| AFJPAM | Air Force joint pamphlet |
| AFV | armored fighting vehicle |
| alt | alternate |
| AM | amplitude modulation |
| AMA | aviation maintenance area |
| AMC | Army Materiel Command |
| ammo | ammunition |
| AO | area of operation |
| assy | assembly |
| atk | attack |
| ATTN | attention |
| AVLB | armored vehicle-launched bridge |
| background | The features in a target area that surround the target. |
| BDU | battle-dress uniform |

blending        A CCD technique that causes a target to appear as part of the background. Many target characteristics must be considered when attempting a blending treatment, including target size and shape, regular patterns in the target scene, and rough or smooth target contours.

| | |
|---|---|
| btry | battery |
| C2 | command and control |

C2W        command and control warfare. The integrated use of PSYOP, military deception, OPSEC, EW, and physical destruction supported by intelligence to deny information to, influence, degrade, or destroy adversary C2 capabilities while protecting friendly C2 capabilities against such actions.

84

C3          command, control, and communications

C3CM         command, control, and communications countermeasure. The integrated use of OPSEC, military deception, jamming, and physical destruction supported by intelligence to deny information to, influence, degrade, or destroy adversary C3 capabilities while protecting friendly C3 capabilities against such actions. camo camouflage. The use of natural or artificial materials on personnel, objects, and tactical positions to confuse, mislead, or evade the enemy.

camouflage net     Part of a system designed to blend a target with its surroundings and conceal the identity of critical assets (aircraft, fixed targets, vehicles, personnel) where natural cover and/or concealment might be absent or inadequate. camouflage net set Standard DOD set consisting of a hexagon-shaped net (673.6 sq ft), a diamond-shaped net (224.5 sq ft), and a net repair kit. camouflage net spreader A plastic or aluminum disc or paddle that is supported by a lightweight pole and used to support camouflage nets above the ground, buildings, or vehicles.

cap          capacity

CB          counterbattery

CCD         camouflage, concealment, and decoys. Methods and resources to prevent adversary observation or surveillance; confuse, mislead, or evade the adversary; or induce the adversary to act in a manner prejudicial to his interests.

CCD treatment     A combination of CCD equipment and techniques applied to a selected target and/or its background to reduce or delay target acquisition. chaff Material consisting of thin, narrow, metallic strips of various lengths and frequency responses used as artificial clouds to scatter radar signals.

clutter         EM radiation from sources around the target that tend to hinder target detection.

CM          countermortar

countermeasure    Any technique intended to confuse or mislead hostile sensors.

COMSEC       communications security

concealment      The protection from observation or surveillance.

conspicuity       A term peculiar to the CCD community that denotes the perceived difference of one feature in a scene as compared to other features in the scene.

corner reflector     An object that reflects multiple signals from smooth surfaces mounted mutually perpendicular and produces a radar return of greater magnitude than expected from the size of the object the reflector conceals.

85

counter-reconnaissance     All measures taken to prevent hostile observation of a force, an area, or a place.

counter-surveillance     All measures, active or passive, taken to counteract hostile surveillance.

cover     Any natural or artificial protection from enemy observation and fire.

covered approach Any route that offers protection against enemy observation or fire.

| | |
|---|---|
| CP | command post |
| CSS | combat service support |
| cu | cubic |
| DA | Department of the Army |
| DC | District of Columbia |

deceive     Any action that causes the enemy to believe the false or purposely causes the enemy to make incorrect conclusions based on false evidence.

deception     Those measures designed to mislead the enemy by manipulation, distortion, or falsification of evidence, inducing him to react in a manner prejudicial to his interests.

decoy     An imitation in any sense of a person, an object, or a phenomenon that is intended to deceive enemy surveillance devices or mislead enemy evaluation.

detection     The discovery of an existence or presence.

disguise     Any alteration of identity cues for items, signals, or systems sufficient to cause misidentification by the enemy.

dispersal     Relocation of forces for the purpose of increasing survivability.

disrupt   Any action intended to interrupt the shape or outline of an object or an individual, making it less recognizable.

| | |
|---|---|
| div | division |
| DLSC | Defense Logistics Service Center |
| DOD | Department of Defense |
| DSN | Defense Switched Network |

ea              each

ECCM            electronic counter-countermeasure. Any action involving effective use of the EM spectrum by friendly forces, despite the enemy's use of EW.

ECM             electronic countermeasure. Any action involving prevention or reduction of an enemy's effective use of the EM spectrum. ECMs include electronic jamming and electronic deception.

electronics security The protection resulting from all measures designed to deny unauthorized persons information of value that, when analyzed, might alert the enemy to the intentions of friendly forces (for example, a signal security provided by encryption equipment).

EM              electromagnetic

EM spectrum     electromagnetic spectrum. The range of frequencies from zero to infinity where energy is transferred by electric and magnetic waves. EM waves at the lower end of this spectrum (low-frequency navigation aids and AM and shortwave radio services) are refracted back to earth by the ionosphere to frequencies as high as 50 MHz At frequencies above 50 MHz, propagation is generally limited to LOS. These frequencies are used by TV, FM radio, and land-mobile and point-to-point communication services. They extend on to parts of the EM spectrum generally termed as radar, IR, visible light, UV light, and cosmic rays.

EW              electronic warfare. Any military action involving the use of EM energy to determine, exploit, reduce, or prevent hostile use of the EM spectrum; action which retains friendly use of the EM spectrum. FAAS-V field artillery ammunition support vehicle

FARP            forward arming and refueling point

FEBA            forward edge of the battle area

fed             federal

FLIRS           Forward-Looking Infrared System. An imaging IR sensor used to acquire a target's heat signature.

FLOT            forward line of own troops

FM              field manual

FM              frequency modulation

FOB             forward operating base

FOD             foreign object damage

fog oil          Petroleum compounds of selected molecular weight and composition to facilitate the formation of smoke by atomization, vaporization, and subsequent recondensation.

FOS          false operating surface. A simulated horizontal construction placed to represent operating surfaces such as runways, taxiways, parking pads, and access roads.

| | |
|---|---|
| freq | frequency |
| ft | foot, feet |
| gal | gallon(s) |
| gen | generator |
| GHz | gigahertz |
| GI | government issue |
| GSR | ground-surveillance radar |

hardening          The construction of a facility to provide protection against the effects of conventional or nuclear explosions. The facility may also be equipped to provide protection against chemical or biological attacks. Construction usually involves reinforced concrete placement and/or burying the structure.

| | |
|---|---|
| HC | hydrogen chloride |
| HEMTT | heavy expanded mobility tactical truck |

hiding          The choice of a position or materials to obstruct direct observation.

| | |
|---|---|
| HMMWV | high-mobility multipurpose wheeled vehicle |
| how | howitzer |
| HQ | headquarters |
| HTF | how to fight |
| HUD | heads-up display |
| HVT | high-value target |

hyperspectral          Refers to a sensor or data with many bands extending over a range of the EM spectrum. imaging radar An electronic or optical process for recording or displaying a scene generated by a radar sensor.

| | |
|---|---|
| in | inch(es) |
| indiv | individual |

intervisibility     The condition of the atmosphere that allows soldiers the ability to see from one point to another. This condition may be altered or interrupted by weather, smoke, dust, or debris.

IPB     intelligence preparation of the battlefield. A systematic approach to analyzing the enemy, weather, and terrain in a specific geographic area. It integrates enemy doctrine with the weather and terrain conditions as they relate to the mission and the specific battlefield environment. IPB provides the framework for determining and evaluating enemy capabilities, vulnerabilities, and probable courses of action.

IR     infrared

IR smoke screen   It produces obscuration in one or more of the transparent IR spectral bands between 0.7 and 14 microns. In most cases, an effective IR smoke screen is also an effective visual smoke screen. However, effective visual smoke screens are not necessarily effective IR smoke screens.

| | |
|---|---|
| JCCD | Joint Camouflage, Concealment, and Deception |
| JSTARS | Joint Surveillance Target Attack Radar System |
| JT&E | Joint Test and Evaluation |
| lb | pound(s) |
| LCSS | Lightweight Camouflage Screen System |
| LLTV | low-light television |
| LOC | lines of communication |
| LOS | line of sight |

low emissivity paint Paint used to lower the apparent temperature of a target (or nearby scene features), thus making the hot target less conspicuous to a thermal target-acquisition sensor. Using a paint that has too low an emissivity (less than 0.6) causes the target to become more visually conspicuous (or shiny).

| | |
|---|---|
| maskirovka | The battlefield doctrine of the former Soviet Union. |
| MCRP | Marine Corps reference publication |
| MCWP | Marine Corps warfighting publication |
| mech | mechanized |
| METT-TC | mission, enemy, terrain, weather, troops, time available, and civilian considerations |
| MHz | megahertz |

mil                military

min                minute(s)

MLRS               Multiple Launch Rocket System

mm                 millimeter(s)

MOUT               military operations on urbanized terrain

movement techniques The methods used by a unit to travel from one point to another (traveling, traveling overwatch, and bounding overwatch) are considered movement techniques. The likelihood of enemy contact determines which technique is used. MTI moving-target indicator

multispectral      Refers to a sensor or data in two or more regions of the EM spectrum.

NA                 not applicable

NBC                nuclear, biological, chemical

NCO                noncommissioned officer

NIR                near infrared

No.                number

NSN                national stock number. A 13-digit number assigned to each item of supply purchased, stocked, or distributed within the federal government.

NVD                night-vision device

NWP                Navy warfighting publication

obsc               obscurant. Suspended particulates or entrained liquid droplets that can absorb and/or scatter EM radiation in various parts of the EM spectrum (visual, IR, radar). obscuration The effects of weather, battlefield dust, and debris; the use of smoke munitions to hamper observation and target acquisition; and the concealment of activities or movement.

OPFOR              opposing forces

OPORD              operation order

OPSEC              operations security. The process of denying adversaries information about friendly capabilities and intentions by identifying, controlling, and protecting signatures associated with planning for and conducting military operations and other activities. It includes counter-surveillance and physical, signal, and information security.

oz                 ounce(s)

POL              petroleum, oils, and lubricants

PSYOP         psychological operations

pub             publication

radar           A device that uses EM waves to provide information on the range, the azimuth, or the elevation of objects. radar camouflage Any radar-absorbing or -reflecting material that changes the radar-echoing properties of an object's surface.

radar clutter      Unwanted signals, echoes, or images displayed by a radar unit that interfere with the observation of desired signals.

radar imagery     The picture produced on a radar screen by recording the EM waves reflected from a given target surface.

radio detection    The detection of a radio's presence by intercepting its signals without precise determination of its position.

radio direction-finding The act of determining the azimuth to a radio transmitter, from a specific location, using signal-detecting equipment.

radio fix         The location of a radio transmitter determined by simultaneously using two direction-finding devices stationed at different locations and plotting the results on a map. The intersection of the two azimuths indicates the transmitter's location.

radio range-finding The act of determining the distance to a radio transmitter. This technique involves using electronic equipment to intercept and measure a transmitter's emissions and then translating this information into a distance.

RAM           radar-absorbing material. Material that absorbs and dissipates incident radar energy as contrasted to radar-scattering material, which reflects the incident energy in a different direction.

RAP           radar-absorbing paint. A coating that can absorb incident radar energy.

RATELO       radiotelephone operator

rckt             rocket

RCS           radar cross section. The size of a conducting square, metal plate that would return the same signal to a radar sensor as a target, provided that the radar energy received at the target is reradiated equally in all directions.

recon        reconnaissance. An exploratory survey of a particular area or airspace by visual, aural, electronic, photographic, IR, or other means. It may imply a physical visit to the area.

redundancy        The use of multiple systems with similar perceived functional capabilities to provide higher system survivability.

relocatable asset   A military asset that normally stays in place for a short period of time relative to a fixed asset.

reverse-slope position A position on the ground that is not exposed to direct fire or observation; for example, a slope that descends away from the enemy.

revetment        A barrier used to protect assets against attack.

ROM        refuel on the move

RSTA        reconnaissance, surveillance, and target acquisition

RT        rough terrain

S&S        supply and service

SAM        surface-to-air missile

SCSPP        standard camouflage screening paint pattern

Scud        A surface-to-surface missile.

signature        Detectable indications that forces are occupying or operating in an area. Signatures can be EM (visible, IR, NIR, radar) or mechanical (acoustic, seismic). Common detectable EM signatures include visible vehicle tracks, thermal flames, and radar signal returns. Common mechanical signatures include radio noise, humans conversing, and seismic ground waves produced by tanks and heavy vehicles.

SLAR        side-looking airborne radar

smk        smoke. An artificially produced aerosol of solid, liquid, or vapor deposited in the atmosphere that inhibits the passage of visible light or other forms of EM radiation.

smky        smoky

smoke generator   A machine that produces large volumes of smoke to support hasty or deliberate operations for screening, protecting, and/or sustaining airfields, ports, staging areas, and bridge crossings. Present smoke generators vaporize liquid aerosol materials such as fog oil, diesel fuel, and polyethylene glycol. These generators consist of a heat source to vaporize the liquid aerosol material and an apparatus for the production of airflow to efficiently disseminate the smoke vapor into the atmosphere where it disperses and condenses. smoke pot An expendable bucket- or pot-like munition that produces dense smoke by burning combustible material.

smoke screen    Smoke generated to deceive or confuse an enemy as to the activities of tactical elements.

SOP             standing operating procedure

SP              self-propelled

sq              square

STANAG          standardization agreement

std             standard

surveillance    A systematic observation of airspace or surface areas by visual, aural, electronic, photographic, IR, or other means. survivability operations Activities involving the development and construction of fighting and protective positions (earth berms, defilade positions, overhead protection, camouflage) that reduce the effectiveness of enemy detection systems.

TAA             tactical assembly area

TACSOP          tactical standing operating procedure

target acquisition  The process involving the detection and identification of hostile operations and equipment for subsequent engagement.

target scene    The view of a target area that includes both the target and its surroundings.

temp            temporary

terrain analysis    The process of examining a geographic area to determine what effects its natural and man-made features may have on military operations.

terrain mottling    A camouflage technique normally used in desert terrain. It involves scarring the earth with heavy equipment to expose patches of bare ground. Equipment and supplies are placed on the bare patches to avoid detection by aerial reconnaissance.

thermal contrast    The difference in radiance (as usually measured in the 8-to-14 micron band) between two features of a scene; for example, a target and its background.

thermal crossover A temporary situation, in the morning or evening, when the target and background temperatures become equal.

thermal emissivity The ratio of the emissive power of a surface to that of a black body. The emissivity is 1 for a black body and 0.9 for most natural and man-made materials. The apparent temperature of a target can be reduced by reducing its real temperature and/or lowering its emissivity. Unfortunately, as the thermal emissivity is lowered, its reflectivity in the visual portion of the spectrum increases, thus making the target more conspicuous to a visual sensor. A typical compromise is 0.7, which lowers the apparent target temperature but does not make it too shiny in the visible spectrum.

| | |
|---|---|
| TM | technical manual |
| TMD | tactical missile defense |

tone down The process of blending a target or other high-value asset with the background by reducing its brightness characteristics using nets or coatings. The recommended reflectance of a target as compared with the surrounding scene is 10 percent or less.

| | |
|---|---|
| TOW | tube-launched, optically tracked, wire-guided |
| TRADOC | United States Army Training and Doctrine Command |
| TV | television |
| UAV | unmanned aerial vehicle |
| US | United States |
| USAES | United States Army Engineer School |
| UV | ultraviolet |
| V | volt |
| w/ | with |
| w/o | without |
| WSA | weapons storage area |
| μ | micron(s) |

# REFERENCES

## Sources Used

These are the sources quoted or paraphrased in this publication. DA Forms are available on the APD website (www.apd.army.mil).

DA Form 2028, Recommended Changes to Publications and Blank Forms.

FM 2-0, Intelligence, 23 March 2010.

FM 3-06. Urban Operations. 26 October 2006.

FM 3-11, Multiservice Tactics, Techniques, and Procedures for Nuclear, Biological, and Chemical Defense Operations, 10 March 2003.

FM 3-25.26, Map Reading and Land Navigation, 18 January 2005.

FM 5-34, Engineer Field Data, 19 July 2005.

FM 5-103, Survivability, 10 June 1985.

FM 21-10, Field Hygiene and Sanitation, 21 June 2000.

JP 1-02, Department of Defense Dictionary of Military and Associated Terms, 23 April 2001.

JP 3-13.1, Electronic Warfare, 23 January 2007.

STANAG 2931 (Edition 2), Orders for the Camouflage of the Red Cross and Red Crescent on Land in Tactical Operations, 19 January 1998.

TM 5-1080-200-13&P, Operator's, Unit, and Direct Support Maintenance Manual (Including Repair Parts and Special Tools List) for Lightweight Camouflage Screen Systems and Support Systems, 29 January 1987.

# Documents Needed

None.

# Readings Recommended

None.

# INDEX

## A

AA. *See* Assembly Area
AAS. *See* Army aviation site
aerial multispectral imagery, 11
aerial recon, 15
Army Aviation Site (AAS), 55
assembly area (AA), 38, 43

## B

background, 45
battle drill, sample of, 75
Battle, CCD during, 40, 46
Blending, 30
By-Products, battlefield, 35

## C

Camouflage items, list of, 80
Camouflage Nets, 33, 44
   modular system, 71
   Module determination chart, 72
Camouflage Requirements & Procedures,
   70
Capabilities, built-in, 58
chlorophyll response, 33, 34
Command Post, 51
communications security (COMSEC), 8
COMSEC. *See* communications security
Counterattack, 42
countermeasures, 21
CP. *See* command post

## D

Data Sources, 32
Deception, 8
Decoying, 30
Defensive Operations, 42

## Desert CCD

Desert CCD, 59
Detection
   avoiding, 20
   routine surveillance, 21
Discipline, 28
Disguising, 30
Disrupting, 30

## E

electromagnetic spectrum, 15
enemy intelligence, 48
Evaluation, 11
Expedient Paint, 34

## F

Flash-sound ranging, 18

## G

Ground-based microphone array, 18

## H

High-Value Targets, 47
   CCD of, 47
   command post, 51
   fixed installation, 49
   planning, 47
   relocatable unit, 57
HVT. *See* High-Value Targets

## I

Image intensifiers, 15
imagery, 15, 24
Individual CCD, 76
infrared (IR), 8
IR. *See* infrared

# L

LLTV. *See* low-light television
Low-light television (LLTV), 15

# M

Maneuver divisions, 14
Materials, use of, 32
medical facilities, camouflage of, 83
Metric Conversion Chart, 64
METT-TC. *See* mission, enemy, terrain, weather, troops, time available, and civilian considerations
mission, enemy, terrain, weather, troops, time available, and civilian considerations (METT-TC), 9
Mobility, 57
Motorized rifle and tank regiments, 14
Movement, 23, 39

# N

Natural Conditions, 31
Natural Materials, 45
NBC. *See* nuclear, biological, chemical
nuclear, biological, chemical (NBC), 8

# O

Obstacles, 45
Offensive Operations, 38
operations security (OPSEC), 8
OPSEC. *See* operations security

# P

Patterns, operational, 24

# R

radar, 14
    counterbattery, 17
    countermortar, 17
    imagin, 17
    moving-target indicators, 17
Radar-Absorbing Material (RAM), 35

RAM. *See* Radar-Absorbing Material
Realistic CCD, 21
Recognition Factors, 24
reconnaissance, surveillance, and target-acquisition (RSTA), 8
remote sensing, 15
reserve forces, 42
RSTA. *See* reconnaissance,

# S

Sensor Systems, 14
    Acoustic, 17
    Hyperspectral, 18
    Infrared, 16
    Multispectral, 18
    Near infrared, 16
    Radio, 18
    Ultraviolet, 16
    Visual, 15
Signatures
    defensive, 42
    offensive, 38
Site Selection, 27
Snow-covered Areas, 60
Special Environments, 59
Supply points, 53
Survivability Positions, 45

# T

TACSOP. *See* Tactical Standing Operating Procedures
Tactical Standing Operating Procedures (TACSOP), 65
Threat, 13

# U

Urban terrain, 27

# V

vegetation, use of, 32
Vehicles, camouflage of, 74

# W

Water Points, 53

By Order of the Secretary of the Army:


GEORGE W. CASEY, JR.
General, United States Army
Chief of Staff


Official:


JOYCE E. MORROW
Administrative Assistant to the
Secretary of the Army
1030803


George J Flynn
Lieutenant General, U.S. Marine Corps
Deputy Commandant for Combat Development and Integration